What is Canadian cuisine? Dozens of cookbook authors and historians have spent decades trying to answer this question, but it turns out that Canadian food isn't summed up by one iconic dish, but rather a huge range of meals, flavours and cultural influences. And for restaurant critic and journalist Gabby Peyton, it's about the people who cooked our food, who gave it to us at lunch counters, in ornate dining rooms and through take-out windows. *Where We Ate* is a celebration of 150 restaurants that have left a mark on the way Canada eats—whether they're serving California rolls, foie gras poutine, hand-cut beef tartare or bánh mì.

Organized chronologically, from pre-Confederation to the present day, you'll be able to flip through the pages and understand how Canadian dining habits evolved from beef consommé at Montreal's Auberge Saint-Gabriel in 1754 to nori-covered hot dogs at Vancouver's Japadog in 2005. Many of the restaurants featured are still open for business, so *Where We Ate* can also act as a guide to the restaurants you want to visit—a book you can pull out again and again whether you're interested in the origin story of Hawaiian pizza or you want to find a place for dinner. In charming, entertaining essays that give cultural, economic and political context, Peyton pays loving homage to each of these unique stalwarts. Paired with transportive photos and menus from archival and personal collections, *Where We Ate* will bring you along on a road trip through some of Canada's most interesting places to eat. For those wishing to truly feel like they're dining in, there are recipes inspired or contributed by some of the featured restaurants.

A joyous representation of the incredible diversity of restaurants, people and stories that make up our Canadian dining history, *Where We Ate* is as much of a timeless classic as the restaurants it features.

Where We Ate

Where We Ate

A Field Guide to Canada's
Restaurants, Past and Present

GABBY PEYTON

appetite
by RANDOM HOUSE

Appetite by Random House® and colophon are registered trademarks of Penguin Random House LLC.

Library and Archives of Canada Cataloguing in Publication is available upon request.

ISBN: 9780525611660
eBook ISBN: 9780525611677

Cover and book design by Emma Dolan
Printed in India

The author acknowledges the support of ArtsNL, which last year invested $3.2 million to foster and promote the creation and enjoyment of the arts for the benefit of all Newfoundlanders and Labradorians.

The author acknowledges the financial support of the Access Copyright Foundation as a Marian Hebb Research Grant recipient.

Published in Canada by Appetite by Random House®, a division of Penguin Random House LLC.
www.penguinrandomhouse.ca

10 9 8 7 6 5 4 3 2 1

To Adam, for everything.

Contents

Foreword

A great frustration of food writing is that once a restaurant has closed, the experience of eating there is forever unavailable.

If you want to hear "Heatwave," by Martha and the Vandellas, you can listen to it right now, in a variety of formats, including the vinyl on which it was originally pressed and sold. Film fans may not be able to find a screening of *Lawrence of Arabia* in 70mm, but they can watch the movie on DVD, Blu-ray, on a streaming site, or even on their phone. Michelangelo's *Creation of Adam* still rests on the ceiling of the Sistine Chapel, where it was painted 400 years ago.

However, if you love restaurants, there is no way to experience any from the past beyond the tangential, peripheral view offered by historical documentation. Unlike other artforms (assuming you, like me, consider restaurants as much a creative medium as commercial enterprise), restaurants are ephemeral. Yes, we have photos, recipes, and menus from century-old restaurants. But the tersely written lists of dishes may as well be hieroglyphics, for all they tell us about what it was like to actually have eaten there. We'll never know the sounds of the street outside, the smells of the room, what it was like to walk from the closest subway station, the view from the window, and so on. Anyone who has bought the vanity cookbook of a celebrity chef, in the hopes of bringing home some part of the memory of dining in that restaurant, knows that the recipes, no matter how exact a blueprint for recreating a signature dish (or convincing you why you shouldn't try it at home), are mere fragments of what it was like to be there.

Having said that, Gabby Peyton has done the next best thing. This book you hold in your hands, while it can never transport us entirely to any one of the restaurants it features, does something that may be more valuable. *Where We Ate* places these restaurants in the periods of their origins—from pre-confederation Canada all the way up until the Instagram-clickbait restaurants of the 2010s—and connects the dots to show us how each era of dining, along with the influences of culinary and immigration trends, flowed into the next.

This book is more than an indulgence of the nostalgic impulse to flip through photos of the olden days, to imagine how we used to eat out, what people wore, or how wide the sidewalks were. *Where We Ate* is a story, told in snack-sized bites, of how Canada went from Turtle Soup to Beef Heart Bolognese.

—Corey Mintz, author of
The Next Supper: The End of Restaurants as We Knew Them, and What Comes After

Have a Seat

You've heard (and probably asked) this question a million times: "Where did you go for dinner?" Sometimes it's the usual spot, the local bistro around the corner. Sometimes it's that vegan place or a new Syrian eatery. Maybe it's the diner that's been around for 50 years (your parents had their first date there).

It's not just about what you ate, but where you ate.

If we are indeed what we eat, we are also shaped by the people who made it for us and where we ate it. And the restaurants in this book have done just that: they have impacted the way we eat. Whether they were the first sushi spot, the first fine-dining establishment, or they changed the way we eat out in Canada altogether, the people who owned these restaurants created the dining culture we know today.

Restaurants are so much more than the iconic food they invent or best-of lists they make. They are a combination of the people who operate them, the atmosphere they create and the food they serve. Restaurants are nothing without

the people who run them and the people who eat there. The families, the friends, the diners—it's all a community.

My happiest childhood memories always took place in a restaurant. On every special occasion, my family went to the Taiwan Restaurant in Grand Falls-Windsor, Newfoundland, where I grew up. For me, it was as good as the idea of a McDonald's PlayPlace (the latter remained an idea, because our hometown didn't get one until I was in my teens and was too big for the ball pit). At the Taiwan, the waterfall trickled into the little rock pond, the fish tank was filled with koi and the beaded curtains concealed private rooms where we would be given hot towels to wipe our hands before the meal. Giant chicken nuggets (sweet-and-sour chicken balls) and a cookie (fortune) at the end of the meal. What more could a kid want?

The Taiwan Restaurant still looks like it did when I was a kid. But through my research for this book, I discovered it didn't always look like an example of

"You've heard (and probably asked) this question a million times: 'Where did you go for dinner?'"

orientalism. I know now that when the restaurant opened in 1964, it didn't have much decoration at all. This led me down a wormhole of research and realization about who that decor was really for.

On opening day, November 10, 1964, a reporter from the local paper, the *Advertiser*, described the two-storey building on High Street. Save for its description of the ceramic tile in green, black and orange with "Taiwan" inscribed in Chinese, and a few lanterns hanging from the ceiling, the article is mostly about the restaurant's trendy terrazzo flooring, garlands of beige drapery and fancy new intercom system. Despite his having emigrated from the Guangdong region of China, sponsored by his father under the family reunion program shortly after Newfoundland joined Canada, it wasn't until 1984, when owner Tom Chow renovated, that he added North Americanized Chinese elements such as ornate carvings of dragons and phoenixes, lanterns, Chinese pagodas and ornate beads closing off the private dining

rooms—it just wasn't part of the Newfoundland restaurant vernacular in the 1960s. Chow's Chinese decor was meant to satisfy the primarily white clientele.

I started working in restaurants in my 20s while finishing my undergrad degree in history at Memorial University of Newfoundland. Even from my position as a server at Get Stuffed in St. John's, I could see how hard everyone worked. The chef, a hired gun who was cooking beneath his talents, fed me sweetbreads and foie gras pâté through the pass, while front-of-house staff taught me all there was to know about liquor orders, how to serve wine and the art of "being there but not being there" when it came to service. With the candles flickering, the soft music playing and the delicious food flying out of the kitchen, I was hooked.

Years later, while writing my monthly series about iconic Canadian foods for *Food Bloggers of Canada*, I delved into our country's culinary history and uncovered the same plotline every time. The origin stories of our early restaurants (and the latest hot spots) all have a place in the Canadian historical compendium. Donairs, California rolls, ginger beef, Japadogs, figgy duff and smoked-meat sandwiches were all invented by those who came to Canada looking for a new life. They built that life by feeding Canadians—both new and old—their traditional recipes, alongside new inventions.

As my food writing career shifted from

blog posts to restaurant reviews as the critic for St. John's only newspaper, the history of restaurants and the people who ran them were always significant to me. It was as important to include the backstory of the owner as it was to rave about their Instagram-worthy dishes. I found myself constantly researching the origin stories of dishes and finding ways to incorporate them into all my freelance work, from writing about long-standing institutions for the *CBC* to talking about the evolution of butter chicken pizza in Canada for my syndicated food trends column.

The more research I did about the history of Canadian restaurants, the more I realized how little has been written. And what's worse is that, somewhere along the way, we lost the culinary narrative. Almost all our restaurant food is immigrant food. Peameal bacon, tourtière and even Montreal-style bagels were all brought here by Europeans. Butter tarts? Brought here by the French. Even bannock, a dish that evokes divisive conversations about colonialism among Indigenous cooks, was brought here by the Scots. Most diners and the mainstream media don't grasp that the dishes tourist brochures and listicles tout as historically Canadian were brought here by immigrants—the English and French settlers who colonized the country (even though our history books don't label them as immigrants).

We often think of geography as the main influence on our food culture— cod is king in Newfoundland, while in Manitoba the wheat kings reign—but we'd be remiss to ignore the social history that makes up our plates, and which is reflected in our restaurants. Countless cookbook authors, historians, chefs, home cooks and academics have spent the better part of the last few decades trying to define Canadian cuisine, which is like trying to define each separate puzzle piece in a thousand-piece jigsaw. It cannot simply be identified by the wild rice and Red Fife wheat, or the plethora of berries, vegetables and wild game making up the mosaic of flavours. For me, Canadian cuisine is about the people who cooked our food, and who gave it to us to eat at lunch counters, at mahogany bars and through take-out windows.

From the first eight hundred French women, known as the King's Daughters, who concocted the recipe for tarte au sucre in 17th-century Quebec, to the new Balkan restaurant churning out chevapi a block from my house in Newfoundland, the arrival of new Canadians (and their recipes) has continually shifted the way we eat. The fabric of our collective history is edible, plated on clunky stoneware at the Jewish deli, chop suey-ed in Chinatown and waltzed around fine-dining ballrooms during the golden age of the department-store luncheon.

The story of Canadian restaurants tells the broader story of the country. Ever wonder why the number of Chinese restaurants exploded in the 1950s? Take Chinese-owned restaurants in Halifax, for example. The first restaurants owned by Chinese immigrants started to appear in the pages of the city's telephone listings in the 1920s but served British dishes under monikers like The North Star Diner. After the repeal of immigration restrictions in 1947, Chinese-named restaurants dominated page after page of Halifax's directory—there were 44 Chinese-owned restaurants by 1952. Chinese restaurants in Nova Scotia shifted from shrimp salad to chop suey, and across the country, Canadians fell in love with egg rolls, fried rice and that fluorescent pink sauce that isn't really Chinese.

When Olympia Pizza owner George Kerasiotis was asked why he opened his Vancouver pizza shop in 1967 after arriving from the Greek island of Evia, his answer was simple: "Every Greek was opening a pizza and pasta place." Fifty years later, there are thousands of pizza shops across the country owned by Greek Canadians, including the inventor of Hawaiian pizza and the founder of Boston Pizza (his name for the eatery was initially Parthenon Pizza).

This work is by no means an encyclopedia nor a complete history of our country's restaurants. It's a love letter. Because the story of Canada's restaurants, and the people who run them, is big. Really big. As of 2022, there were seventy thousand restaurants across the country. I'm hopeful that this book will provide a spotlight on the thousands of people who opened restaurants and changed the landscape of our dining scene, even if we didn't notice while we were slurping on those noodles and shovelling in those french fries. While I made significant effort to include restaurants of all backgrounds, there are many cultures and communities not included in the book for myriad reasons, whether it be a lack of record-keeping by small business owners, biased census takers or racist business practices which would have obstructed minorities from owning businesses or finding employment. The conspicuous lack of Indigenous restaurants until chapter 13 is also part of our restaurant history; a consequence of systemic racism towards Indigenous people in Canada ranging from prohibitive game laws to forced assimilation.

For the ease of the reader, the book is organized chronologically by decade. But like most history books, the history of restaurants in Canada and their trends blur over time and plate. In addition to conducting dozens of personal interviews with journalists, chefs and restaurant owners, I've scoured old directories, newspapers and menus to create a picture of the evolution of restaurants in this country, but also to give a face and story to all the people who came here and opened restaurants. Each of these chapters is a snapshot of dining in Canada, a moment of enjoyment and nourishment captured. Here's where we ate.

…pital of Upper Canada on the Bay of Toronto in Lake On…

CHAPTER ONE

Before Confederation

"The term 'restaurant' didn't enter the modern vernacular in France until the mid-18th century, as a derivative of the verb *restaurer*, meaning to restore oneself."

Before the marriage proposals, the Instagrammable Caesars piled high with garnishes, the best-of lists, the televised cooking competitions, the family dinners, and the free pieces of cake on your birthday, it still mattered where you ate. Between the arrival of European settlers in the 1400s through to the 1700s, there were few restaurants, hotels or even cities for that matter, but everyone still had to eat. In Canada, when it came to any whisper of "dining," those who did eat out of the house ate simple meals at long public tables in poorly cleaned boarding homes. Eating was for sustenance, not for pleasure or pastime, especially when compared with Europe, where the concept of dining was already in practice. But considering that the term "restaurant" didn't enter the modern vernacular in France until the mid-18th century, as a derivative of the verb *restaurer*, meaning to restore oneself, it probably shouldn't come as a surprise that the best-of list for Montreal restaurants wasn't very long when that city of fewer than five hundred inhabitants resided in a cluster of houses adjacent to a windmill.

Public dining was also political in the 1700s as Loyalists left America, spreading throughout the Maritimes and Southern Ontario, while the Mennonites arrived from Pennsylvania. As the War of 1812 raged on, the first pubs, inns and eating establishments sprouted up along the Great Lakes in what would one day be Canada and served pints of beer, glasses of whisky and heavy plates of meat and potatoes in addition to being community hubs. Some of these establishments continue to exist today.

By the mid-19th century, dining in public was the by-product of travel as thousands of émigrés from around the world passed through the ports at Quebec and Halifax. Before the 1850s, there was no railway, so the inns and taverns found every few miles or so were a haven for those travelling to newly acquired farmland on the Prairies, to a new job as a logger in a camp in Upper Canada or across Vancouver Island on the hunt for gold. In the cities, fine-dining establishments served roast beef, wild game and puddings influenced by French and British chefs on fine bone china, while the select few in high society who could dine out listened to the piano in the corner beneath crystal chandeliers.

Auberge Saint-Gabriel

MONTREAL, QUEBEC (1754–Present)

The first liquor licence in North America was granted to a restaurant still in operation today. In 1688, a retired French soldier named Étienne Truteau built his private residence on rue Saint-Gabriel, one of the first streets in Montreal, when the city was merely a small collection of fortified buildings. Richard Dulong took over the property in 1754, turning it into an inn and landed himself the very first liquor licence under British rule: *"Richard Dulong is licenfe to keep a publik Ale-Houfe, or Victuallking houfe, and to tutter and fell frong Liquors by Retail, for one whole Year, tp be computed from the Twenty-fifth Fay of March 1769."*

The Auberge Saint-Gabriel has had at least a dozen owners since Dulong started serving up those ales, and at least a dozen names over the centuries: Hotel Sant-Louis, Hotel Ridendeau, Hotel Franco-Canadien, the Cecil Hotel and the Grand Hotel. Finally, Ludger Truteau bought the hotel in 1914, called it Auberge Saint-Gabriel and started serving beef consommés and veal with mushrooms. In the mid-20th century, it became a hangout for judges, lawyers and newspaper reporters, known to them affectionately as the Old St. Gabe. The Bolay family took over in 1987, and these days, owners Marc Bolay and Garou and Guy Laliberté skew Mediterranean with their menu, using local ingredients and serving it up in the low-ceilinged stone house with wooden beams. There's even a tunnel that was once used to connect the house to a trading post and which now leads to a speakeasy, a somewhat paradoxical choice for a spot that's held a liquor licence longer than Canada has been a country.

Swiss Fondue

Recipe from
Auberge Saint-Gabriel

The fondue by the current owner of the centuries-old Auberge Saint-Gabriel, Marc Bolay, has been a staple on the cold-weather menu at this Montreal institution for more than 15 years now. Every autumn they bring back their unctuous Swiss fondue, served with roasted potatoes and lardons, cured meats and tons of cubed baguette just begging to be dipped. A bottle of cold Champagne sweating alongside this cuts the richness and adds a touch of luxury to an otherwise simple dish.

SERVES 6 TO 8

2 cloves garlic, halved

¾ cup (185 ml) white or sparkling wine

5 cranks of the pepper mill, or to taste

6¼ cups (700 g) grated Gruyère

2¼ cups (300 g) diced Vacherin Fribourgeois

1 Tbsp (15 ml) cornstarch

1 tsp (5 ml) brandy

1 tsp (5 ml) baking soda

2 baguettes, cut into cubes

1. Rub the cut sides of the garlic halves on the inside of an enamel fondue pot.

2. Add the wine and fresh ground pepper and bring to a simmer on the stovetop over medium-high heat.

3. Immediately add the Gruyère, Vacherin Fribourgeois and cornstarch. Mix gently until the cheese is completely melted and smooth.

4. When the mixture begins to bubble lightly at the sides, mix the brandy and baking soda together in a small bowl, then pour over the cheese and gently combine.

5. As soon as the cheese foams, transfer the fondue pot to a warmer.

6. Enjoy immediately with cubed baguette, and any other dipping foods you desire.

Olde Angel Inn

NIAGARA-ON-THE-LAKE, ONTARIO (1789–Present)

Legend has it that after Lieutenant-Governor John Graves Simcoe signed the Act to Limit Slavery in Upper Canada on July 9, 1793, he and other legislators dined at the Harmonious Coach House in the then capital of Upper Canada, Newark (now Niagara-on-the-Lake, Ontario). Although it took decades for slavery to be completely abolished in Canada, the coach house was a centre of politics and dining at the beginning of the 19th century. Things were not so harmonious when retreating American soldiers razed the inn during the War of 1812. John Ross rebuilt the inn in 1815 and called it the Olde Angel Inn, a compliment to his wife whom he adored.

Today, the inn serves up British pub favourites and is frequented by tourists and by ghost hunters looking to connect with a soldier who died in the fire. The inn is a self-proclaimed hot spot, with sightings of the ghost (detected by motion sensor) as recently as 2020.

l'Hôtel de la Nouvelle Constitution

QUEBEC CITY, QUEBEC (1792)

The first restaurant in the colony of New France didn't last long. It was opened by Charles-René Langlois, the former cook of the Lieutenant-Governor of Lower Canada, Alured Clarke. Poignantly named after the French constitution that was signed in 1791 and intending to lure in new residents to the city of Quebec, it lasted only six months because, frankly, there wasn't anyone around to eat in restaurants.

King's Head Inn

BURLINGTON BAY, ONTARIO (1794–1813)

If you had made your way along rural roads at the turn of the century, you'd see the inns and taverns that were the way-marks for new arrivals to Upper Canada. Save for the small wooden sign each had outside, they all looked the same: a two-storey Georgian home, perfectly symmetrical, with clapboard siding. Transportation inland of any kind was minimal (the railway didn't start operating until the 1850s), so these hubs became a lifeline for people; there was probably one every mile or two along major roadways in what would eventually become Southern Ontario.

The King's Head Inn on Burlington Bay, also known as Government House, was one of the state-owned inns that Lieutenant-Governor John Graves Simcoe had built to facilitate travel. Like the architecture, the menus didn't differ drastically among these inns. Breakfast was simple and might include fried pork and buckwheat cakes, while lunch con-sisted primarily of roast beef or pork and sometimes wild game, with recipes adapted from the ones cooks exchanged with First Nations peoples, along with vegetables and pudding and sometimes wild rice. Dinner was a simpler affair: leftovers from lunch. There were always glasses of whisky or brandy, pints of beer and lots of hot tea. Most interestingly, many of the inns didn't discriminate when it came to mealtimes; those of all classes, races and genders would have eaten side by side at the inns of Upper Canada.

The King's Head Inn from the North-West Burlington Bay

Toronto Coffee House

TORONTO, ONTARIO (1801–1806)

Serial entrepreneur William Cooper arrived in York in 1792 from Bath, England, and in 1801 he opened Toronto Coffee House. It was the first establishment to use "Toronto" in its name, and the first to reference coffee houses. His ad in the *Upper Canada Gazette* described the Georgian-style two-storey house, noting that "nothing shall be wanting on his part to place it as nearly on the footing of an English Inn as local circumstances permit." Like many taverns in Upper Canada at the beginning of the 19th century, it was all about the bed, the booze and the food, and Cooper aimed to live up to the standards of European accommodations. He offered the best wines, brandy, gin and porter beers from London in addition to cigars, pipes and tobacco. The daily menu offered up anchovies, red herring and oysters.

See image, page 8: Coopers Coffee House, York, Upper Canada (Wording FPO)

Restaurant Compain

MONTREAL, QUEBEC (1847–1891)

Sebastien Compain's restaurant was about to make a lot of turtle soup. On July 8, 1890, the *Gazette* reported that the biggest green turtle ever brought to Montreal, weighing in at 458 pounds, was in Compain's possession. The restaurateur had big plans for it. Dealing with high volumes of meat was nothing new to the former mess chef who cooked for two brigades of riflemen and the 77th Regiment, as well as for several private clubs across the city where the most celebrated gourmands broke bread.

His Restaurant Compain, situated inside the Cosmopolitan Hotel right at the Place D'Armes, had burnt down in the 1860s, but his new location at 118 rue Saint-Françoise-Xavier was said to be one of the best in the city, featuring West Indies Turtle, in both soups and steaks.

Cosmopolitan Hotel, Place D'Armes, Montreal

Windsor House Hotel

OTTAWA, ONTARIO (1850s–1957)

The two men, Thomas Ahearn and Warren Soper, responsible for putting electric lighting in the Parliament Buildings, were also responsible for the first full meal ever prepared in an electric range oven in the world. A party of one hundred—invited personally by the hotel's owner, Mr. Daniels—included local celebrities like Mayor Olivier Durocher and the presidents of Ottawa Electric Railway and Chaudière Electric Light and Power.

The menu on August 29, 1892, featured more than 20 items, ranging from consommé royal to sugar-cured ham with Champagne sauce, and oven-cooked items like beef sirloin with horseradish, lamb cutlets with green peas, strawberry puffs and apple soufflés doused in a wine sauce, all of which no doubt would have taken the cooks days to complete without the electric oven.

At the end of the meal, Ahearn took his guests to his company's shed nearby, where the meal had been prepared in a six-by-six-foot brick oven with large glass peepholes that allowed them a glimpse at the future of dining.

Left: View of Windsor House Hotel, 1957

Six Mile Pub

VICTORIA, BRITISH COLUMBIA (1855–Present)

The Sooke gold rush of 1864 might have ended quickly in a trickle, but the road-houses created to satiate weary travellers lived on for a long time. Six Mile Pub, which now has 24 taps and an idyllic Tudor exterior, was once a small wooden structure built by sawmill owner John Fenton. Bill Parsons, a former London bobby, took over the sawmill from Fenton in 1848 after he gallivanted off to participate in the California gold rush. Parsons proceeded to buy 40 acres from the Hudson's Bay Company and built a hotel, and a bridge to access it.

Inside the Parsons Bridge Hotel was Six Mile Pub, named for the dropping-off points for coaches along the road—the hotel is exactly six miles from Victoria on the way to Sooke and the now-abandoned Leechtown, which was a boomtown during the gold rush. Six Mile Pub continued to be a useful source of sustenance for the British soldiers of Esquimalt naval base, who filled up their barrels in the mill's stream and prospered with covert booze sales during Prohibition. These days, they have a wide selection of items on the menu, and you can still visit other gold rush road-houses: 17 Mile Pub in Sooke, and the Four Mile Brewpub & Brewery, which is, you guessed it, two miles up the road.

Stewart's Dining Room & Oyster Saloon

HALIFAX, NOVA SCOTIA (1857–1865)

While the Prince of Wales (later, King Edward VII) was completing his tour of Canada and the United States in the summer of 1860, William Stewart was preparing his kitchen to cater an important pitstop. As one of the dining saloons that lined Bedford Row and Hollis Street in pre-confederation Halifax, he offered up catering on the HMS *Neptune*, which would float alongside other boats during the regatta held in honour of the prince's visit, as those eager to catch a glimpse of the prince watched as he sailed into town. He also constructed a pavilion in front of

his restaurant, also known as the Head Quarters, at the corner of Prince and Hollis, which is now the Snug portion of the Olde Triangle Pub.

Like most saloons in the 1860s, it was all about the oysters—Little Necks, Rockaway, Blue Point, Buzzard Bay and Cape Cod Oysters—and they were served in myriad ways: on the half shell with hot sauce or some scrapings of horseradish, but also made into soup, patties and puddings, or stewed, curried, baked, à la poulette, and, of course, fried.

Fried Oysters

Recipe inspired by
Stewart's Dining Room
& Oyster Saloon

The latter half of the 19th century was the golden age of oysters. With advancements in food preservation and transportation that allowed oysters to be carried across the country, along with a major surge in agricultural production, they showed up seemingly everywhere. They were the cheap, fast and trendy food of the day. This recipe has been updated for modern enjoyment, swapping out the lard used for frying with vegetable oil. Serve with your favourite dipping sauce—a garlicky aioli works great.

1. Shuck the oysters, pat them dry and set aside.

2. In a large bowl, beat the eggs with a splash of cold water. Stir in the salt and pepper.

3. Spread the cracker crumbs on a shallow plate.

4. Dip each oyster in the egg mixture, shaking off any excess, then roll in the crumbs to evenly coat. Set aside on a baking sheet to dry for a few minutes.

5. Heat the oil in a deep frying pan or Dutch oven to 350°F (175°C). In batches, carefully add the coated oysters and fry until the exteriors are golden brown, about 2 minutes. Make sure to let the oil come up to temperature between batches.

6. Transfer the oysters to a plate lined with paper towel to drain. Serve while still warm.

SERVES 2

1 dozen fresh oysters

2 eggs

½ tsp (2 ml) kosher salt

¼ tsp (1 ml) freshly ground black pepper

1 cup (250 ml) crumbled crackers, dried breadcrumbs, or panko, for dredging

Vegetable oil, for frying (about 2 cups/500 ml)

Pioneer Hotel

CAMERONTON, BRITISH COLUMBIA (1864–1870)

British Columbia's Interior during the Cariboo gold rush in the late 19th century focused on striking it rich, and with that came a series of bakeries, saloons and restaurants in the towns founded by gold hunters. Just down the creek from "bustling" Barkerville, the biggest of the four towns along Williams Creek at the end of the Cariboo Road, was the Pioneer Hotel, the oldest hotel in Cameronton, known for its clean beds and efficient cooks. Those hungry after a morning of prospecting or striking it poor could nourish themselves at Mrs. Janet Allen's hotel, which served a full dinner every day at 11:30 a.m.

Otherwise known as Scotch Jeannie, Mrs. Allen was a well-known hotelier who opened several establishments along the Cariboo Road and was recognized for her delicious plum pudding. In 1865, for $1.50, patrons could dine on a feast of oyster soup, roasted pork with a green-apple sauce, pickled tongue with cabbage and plum pudding and green rhubarb pie, and then wash it down with a tea, coffee, milk, cider or lager beer, included in the price. Unfortunately, that only lasted until the town was deserted in 1870.

Left: Pioneer Hotel Mosquito Creek, B.C. after Janet Allen moved the hotel from Camerontown. Donald Rankin, Mrs. Janet Allen and James Rankin posed in front of the hotel.

CHAPTER TWO

Confederation to 1910

"The development of the transnational railway sped up as the culture of restaurants slowed down."

After the confederation of Canada in 1867, the development of the transnational railway sped up as the culture of restaurants slowed down, turning dining out into a pastime of the elite. The construction and completion of the Canadian National Railway in 1885 had fuelled the arrival of thousands of immigrants, particularly Chinese and Italian, and was the catalyst for the rise of the castle-like Canadian Pacific hotels, and on the Prairies Ukrainians arrived—some 170,000 between 1891 and the First World War. These iconic hotels motivated more Canadians to travel and eat out, and restaurant dining became an acceptable, if not a demanded, part of high society. Meanwhile, the lower classes dined in the dozens of offshoot hotels and cafes along the rail lines that fed the train porters, the cleaners and the railway workers. Even the smallest Prairie towns of 50 people would have a restaurant.

The 1900s ushered in a new era of dining as restaurants moved out of hotels and inns and became separate, stand-alone eating spaces. Where we ate started to matter, as it was the wealthy who chose to eat out, whereas working classes were forced to out of necessity. The British tradition of afternoon tea cemented itself into the culture in Victoria, British Columbia, and across the country, while French food remained the idealized high-end cuisine, with dishes like consommé a la brunoise, imported caviar and chicken fricassee. The saloons and oyster bars that had once dominated city directories were now side by side with cafes, tearooms and lunch counters. The big cities saw the first large department stores, which would later become popular with "ladies who lunch," as well as the quick lunch counter. Those small eating establishments, typically with only a few stools at a counter, were open 24 hours a day and filled with working-class urbanites consuming big breakfasts, sandwiches and lots of tea and coffee.

Washington's Restaurant

SAINT JOHN, NEW BRUNSWICK (1879–1911)

After a show at the Union Street Opera House, Washington's Restaurant would always fill up. In the late 1800s, Charlotte Street in Saint John was the social and leisure hub of the port city, and Thomas C. Washington, who also started the first Black baseball club in New Brunswick, was at the centre of it. Oyster suppers were popular, and in 1891, the New York City transplant installed electricity to keep the treats from his new ice cream parlour, which showcased vanilla, lemon, strawberry, ginger, pistachio and pineapple flavours, deliciously cold.

Joe's Juneau

DAWSON CITY, YUKON (1899–1900)

Joe Juneau is known to be one of the most famous prospectors during the Klondike gold rush, but before his death, he owned a small restaurant in Dawson City—and, word has it, was darn good at making sourdough bread. His restaurant was known for being one of the best sourdough saloons that populated the town at the beginning of the 20th century. To this day, sourdough is an important part of the dining culture in Yukon, a result of the prospectors who brought the starters along with them to the northern territories and Alaska during the gold rushes (conventional leavening agents like yeast didn't work well in colder climates, and even sourdough starters were a challenge; prospectors would even sleep with theirs to keep them warm and alive).

When B.F. Germain took over Joe's Juneau at the corner of Second Avenue and Third Street in the summer of 1900, a year after Juneau had died, the *Dawson Daily News* reported that "when a man came in from the creeks, tired and hungry, he was most liable to drift into the old sourdough restaurant for a big square meal." And they went to Joe's Juneau.

Top: Front Street
Dawson, July 1899
Bottom: Wannakers
Restaurant, September
1912, formerly
Washington's Restaurant

Canadian Pacific Hotels, Glacier House

GLACIER NATIONAL PARK, BRITISH COLUMBIA (1887–1929)

At a Royal Geographical Society meeting in London, England, in October 1889, Rev. W. Spotswood Green gave a talk about his recent adventure in the Canadian Rockies. Revealing his lantern-lit slides of snow-capped mountains, valleys filled with majestic glaciers and rushing torrents that were reachable only by train, he raved of the beauty at Glacier House, a "charming inn," and the meal he ate there.

News of the Glacier House experience spread fast after it had opened for business in 1886, with articles in the *Los Angeles Times* and the *New York Times* praising the train journey to dine there. Swiss mountaineers were employed to guide tourists, and opulent breakfasts, lunches and dinners were served onboard to wealthy travellers as they enjoyed sprawling views of the Selkirk Mountains. What was initially a dining stop between Vancouver and Calgary became a dining destination—all because dining cars were too heavy to make it up the mountain.

Glacier House had a horrible demise in the 1920s when an avalanche tore through Rogers Pass, killing more than 50 people. All that's left of it is a small stone monument, but its legacy lives on at the Château Lake Louise and Banff Springs Hotel.

Left: Glacier House exterior, 1892

Banff Springs Hotel

BANFF, ALBERTA (1888–Present)

It took Cornelius Van Horne seven years to realize his architectural dreams at the Banff Springs Hotel, the first of the grand Canadian Pacific hotels, beginning with its inception in 1881 and ending with the hotel's completion in 1888. Little did he know it would set the architectural standard for a hotel empire, along with the Parliament Buildings in Ottawa, which all possess the iconic château-like features renowned the world over, even today.

What started as a five-storey wooden structure designed by architect Bruce Price became, by the early 1900s, a world-famous hotel catering to wealthy international travellers. In the hotel's first dining room, called the Alberta Dining Room, adventure-seeking tourists from as far away as South Africa dined on celery en branche, corned pork a la macedoine and prime rib with browned potatoes after a day of mountaineering, canoeing or golfing. In 1972, head bartender Peter Fich invented the B-52 shot there by layering Kahlua, Baileys and Grand Marnier.

Château Frontenac

QUEBEC CITY, QUEBEC (1893–Present)

When Quebec City residents call the hotel to make a reservation, many still just refer to it as "the Dining Room," even though it's been called the Champlain since the 1990s. As one of the most prestigious hotels in Canada, the Château Frontenac has a long history of fine dining—everyone from Charles de Gaulle to Grace Kelly has dined there—and there have always been several places to eat. When the hotel first opened in 1893, there was the dining room, the drawing room where men could smoke cigars and a tearoom for ladies. The Pink Room was the main place for afternoon tea and was also the location for the secret Quebec Conferences in 1943 and 1944; British prime minister Winston Churchill would have appreciated the scones while discussing military strategies with his allies Franklin D. Roosevelt and William Lyon Mackenzie King.

The dining room's menu from day one was French: Chef Henry Journet, who ran the kitchen in the presidential house, was imported from France. Like the restaurants of most Quebec inns, Château Frontenac's has always featured cheese; on the September 9, 1930, dinner menu there were at least 16 types of cheese to choose from (the imported Roquefort for 45 cents, for instance, or the beloved hometown favourite, Oka, for 30 cents) after a dinner of grilled Gaspé salmon, American-style, or roast lamb with mint sauce.

These days, the Fairmont group has made it one of the most prestigious places to eat in the city and, of course, there's a massive cheese cave with glass walls for everyone to see. Start with beautifully crafted cocktails in the circular-roomed 1608 Bar, then head into Champlain Restaurant, overlooking the city and St. Lawrence River, with its five-course tasting menu highlighting hare stew with pumpkin ravioli, Quebec foie gras, and roasted duck and caribou. The dishes flow from the kitchen beneath the 1920s painted ceiling featuring both a rose and a fleur-de-lys, to represent England and France.

The Champlain Restaurant dining room at Fairmont Le Château Frontenac

McAdam Railway Station

MCADAM, NEW BRUNSWICK (1901–1979)

The McAdam Railway Station hotel started as a waypoint, connector accommodation for luxury travellers headed to The Algonquin Resort via train at McAdam Junction. Like the other château-style CP hotels, it was built, in 1901, in the grand château style, only smaller. Seventeen rooms accommodated overnight guests, while the ornate dining room serviced the first-class passengers, and the lunch counter served a quick bite to the lower-class train passengers. Until the early 1990s, any train traveller headed into the Maritimes would make their way through McAdam Junction, where weary travellers would dig into the famous "railway pie"—newspapers as far away as Boston raved about the circular desserts even in the early days.

The formal dining room closed in 1959, followed by the lunch counter in 1979. But in 1994, when the hotel was turned into a museum, the ovens got hot again. Railway Pie Sundays started in 2010, and visitors sidled up to the huge M-shaped lunch counter, which was added in 1911, and at its peak, it fed twelve hundred people arriving from Montreal or Boston per day. On summer Sunday afternoons from 2010 to 2020, guests could sample some of the 24 pies on offer, from Apple Caramel Pecan or Hawaiian Rhubarb to Lemon Meringue or Key Lime, made by four local women, two of whom were in their 90s.

Bottom: The famous M-shaped lunch counter

Apple Caramel Pecan Pie

Recipe from the McAdam Railway Station

Railway Pie Sundays lasted for almost a decade. This pie is Frank Campbell's favourite. Campbell is a director of the McAdam Historical Restoration Commission and co-founder of the event; the pie was created by his wife, Agnes Campbell, another co-founder and one of four women who pumped out more than 60 pies every week.

1. Preheat the oven to 425°F (220°C).

2. Place the flour and shortening in a large bowl and, using a pastry blender, work the shortening into the flour until they come together in pea-sized pieces. There should be no flour left in the bowl once it's worked in.

3. Add the cold water and toss very lightly. The more you handle the dough at this stage, the tougher the crust will be.

4. Divide the dough into two balls and roll each out to a 12-inch (30 cm) diameter. Gently transfer one crust to a 9-inch (23 cm) pie plate, making sure to work the dough into the edges of the pan and up the sides. There will be some overhang.

5. Sprinkle the finely chopped pecans over the bottom crust (use just enough to make a single layer).

6. Add the sliced apples to the pie plate until it won't hold any more (don't worry, the apples will shrink during baking).

MAKES ONE 9-INCH (23 CM) PIE

2 cups (500 ml) all-purpose flour

1 cup (250 ml) shortening, cubed

¼ cup (60 ml) cold water

¼ cup (60 ml) finely chopped pecans

6 large apples, peeled and sliced

¼ cup (60 ml) packed brown sugar

Cinnamon powder

⅓ cup (80 ml) caramel sauce, store-bought or homemade, plus more to taste

¼ cup (60 ml) chopped pecans, for topping

7. Pat a thin layer of brown sugar overtop the apples, then sprinkle a thin layer of cinnamon.

8. Top with the second crust, and crimp or use a fork to seal the edges, trimming any overhang. Cut slits in the top crust to allow steam to escape during baking.

9. Place the pie on a baking sheet lined with aluminum foil to catch any drips during baking.

10. Bake for 35 to 45 minutes, or until the crust is golden and the apples are tender.

11. While the pie is still warm, drizzle with the caramel sauce, covering most of the crust with a thin layer. Sprinkle with the chopped pecans.

12. Serve warm, or allow the pie to cool to room temperature first.

Royal Alexandra Hotel

WINNIPEG, MANITOBA (1906–1967)

For more than 30 years, Chef Lucien Schickele headed up the kitchen at the Royal Alexandra Hotel in Winnipeg, carefully crafting menus filled with Calf's Liver Dumplings with Glazed Bacon and Noodles Grand'Mere (70 cents), Salmi (a stew) of Duckling with Cherries ($1) and Stewed Finnan Haddie and Oysters with Curry and Boiled Rice (85 cents). From the day it opened its doors in 1906 until 1939, the hotel was his life—he even married the coffee shop manager, E.J. Baxter, in 1935; they had their wedding dinner in the hotel's Windsor Room.

In addition to coining the name for a local fish—the "Lake Winnipeg Gold-eye," as it's still known today— Schickele helped form the crafts of dozens of chefs who eventually moved on to head up kitchens in Canadian Pacific hotels across the country. Before moving on to cook in their own kitchens, chefs were sent to Schickele by Canadian Pacific Railway to ensure they were up to its high standards. On his last day of service, in 1939, the menu wasn't particularly celebratory, "just good, tasty food."

Left: The Grill Room/Cafe

Empress Hotel

VICTORIA, BRITISH COLUMBIA (1908–Present)

The Palm Room at Fairmont's Empress Hotel was where afternoon tea was taken, and to be seen there was just as important as the food itself. The Tea Lobby started serving tea in 1908, when the hotel opened, but in 1928 the service shifted into the Palm Room, where beneath the stained-glass dome Victoria's elite sipped tea and gossiped. It was the city's women who proposed moving the famous afternoon tea back into the lobby, after it was discovered that the acoustics in the Palm Room were so good, their scandalous scuttlebutt could be heard straight across the room. Today, the clink of silverware against custom-made china cups reverberates a little less among the classical columns and tall palms that dot the lobby lounge of the Empress Hotel as more than four hundred sippers a day take part in this bucket-list experience.

Clockwise from top:
Tea in the Lobby Lounge,
1950; A view of the
Empress from Victoria
Harbor; Afternoon Tea
outside the Empress

Signature Raisin Scones

Recipe from the Fairmont Empress Hotel

Any good afternoon tea needs to have these three elements: dainty sandwiches, sweet pastries and, of course, scones. For more than a century, the Empress has been serving the tea-time trifecta and, since 2000, when the Fairmont took over operations, it's been serving these raisin scones, which must be accompanied by the requisite clotted cream and a slather of strawberry jam. Make sure to chill all your ingredients before mixing, for best results.

1. In a medium bowl, whisk together the cream and 1 egg.

2. In a separate bowl, sift the flour sugar, baking powder and salt.

3. Using a pastry cutter or your fingers, work the butter into the flour mixture until they come together in pea-sized pieces. Take care not to overmix. If the butter starts to feel warm, place the entire bowl in the freezer for it to firm up.

4. Add the cream mixture to the flour mixture, along with the raisins, and knead with your hands, working the dough as little as possible. If you have time, place the dough in the fridge or freezer to rest for about 10 minutes before rolling out.

5. On a well-floured work surface using a floured rolling pin, roll the dough into a ¾-inch- (2 cm) thick circle.

MAKES 8 SCONES

½ cup (125 ml) 35% cream

2 eggs, divided

1 cup (250 ml) all-purpose flour

¼ cup (60 ml) granulated sugar

1 Tbsp (15 ml) baking powder

Pinch of salt

¼ cup (60 ml) unsalted butter, cubed

¼ cup (60 ml) golden raisins

2 Tbsp (30 ml) 2% milk

6. Cut the dough into eight evenly sized wedges, and place them on a lightly greased baking sheet.

7. Allow the scones to rest for 45 minutes in the refrigerator while preheating the oven to 325°F (160°C).

8. Whisk the remaining 1 egg with the milk, and brush the scones just before baking with the egg wash.

9. Bake on the middle rack of the oven for 18 to 22 minutes, or until golden brown.

Sing Tom's Cafe

TORONTO, ONTARIO (1901–1902)

Found among ramshackle buildings clad with English and Chinese signs in The Ward, Sing Tom's Cafe was the first Chinese restaurant in Toronto. Its opening coincided with the beginning of the first Chinatown in the city running along York and Elizabeth Streets between Dundas West and Queen West, just east of where today's Chinatown bustles with fruit vendors, noodle slurpers and crockery sellers.

Sing Tom's Cafe was replaced by Kong Yee Teas in 1902, and other restaurants, like Hung Fah Low and Jung Wah, became popular with both Chinese and Jewish residents of The Ward. Just a few years later, in 1908, the City made it illegal for white women to work in Chinese-owned establishments and also made it illegal for establishments to sell alcohol, which spurred the service of "cold tea," supplied in ornate china teapots to imbibers.

Cafe Aagaard

BRANDON, MANITOBA (1902–1921)

Cafe Aagaard was the place for oysters at the turn of the 20th century in Brandon, Manitoba. Despite the cafe's proximity to the CPR station, how anyone would have been able to attain fresh oysters from Baltimore in landlocked Manitoba will forever remain a mystery. But the Aagaard brothers, Walter and Tenney, born in Minnesota of Danish parents, even put ads in the *Brandon Sun* proclaiming one should eat oysters only at their restaurant, because "they are direct from Baltimore, select, they are fresh, they are large and fat."

The brothers were certainly concerned about temperature, as per their 1917 ad where they talked about how it wasn't just the food they served and whether it was clean that was important, but it was also the small details of service and temperature. The formal dining room upstairs with crystal water jugs, French bistro tables and white tablecloths boasted a no-tip policy, the first in Brandon to do so. The downstairs lunch counter was more informal, offering up large plates of breakfast ranging in price from 15 to 35 cents. The big breakfast at 35 cents consisted of "Half-Orange, Breakfast Cereal or Porridge and Cream, one Egg or Bacon or Ham, and Toast or Rolls, and Coffee, Tea or Milk." And I'd be remiss not to mention their slogan: "Our Breakfast Coffee is a Bracer."

Cafe Aagaard, interior

Wood's West End Candy Store

ST. JOHN'S, NEWFOUNDLAND & LABRADOR (1902–1923)

When Frederick B. Wood opened his flagship store at 348–350 Water Street in January 1902, it was a big upgrade from his small fruit and confectionery shop just up the street. A large two-storey building with a brick rotunda loomed over Water Street. The first floor was filled with confections from Wood's Henry Street candy factory: jams, jellies, spices and aerated waters, not to mention bins of Florida oranges and grapes. The smell of peanuts wafted through the air.

Upstairs, starched servers whisked around the formal dining room that was adorned with lace curtains, potted palms and a pressed-tin ceiling, serving the elite of St. John's mutton pies and oysters on the half shell. It was the place to be seen taking tea and became so fashionable that the local newspapers came round to report just who was eating there. On March 18, 1905, the *Evening Telegram* reported, "Many of the prominent residents of Bell Island came to the city yesterday and had a dinner at Wood's restaurant. They were served in excellent manner with all the dainties of the season and had a thoroughly enjoyable afternoon." So popular was Wood's culinary endeavours that he opened two more locations.

In 1923, after Wood retired, W.R. Goobie purchased the confection section and turned it into Purity Factories, now one of Newfoundland and Labrador's most recognizable food brands.

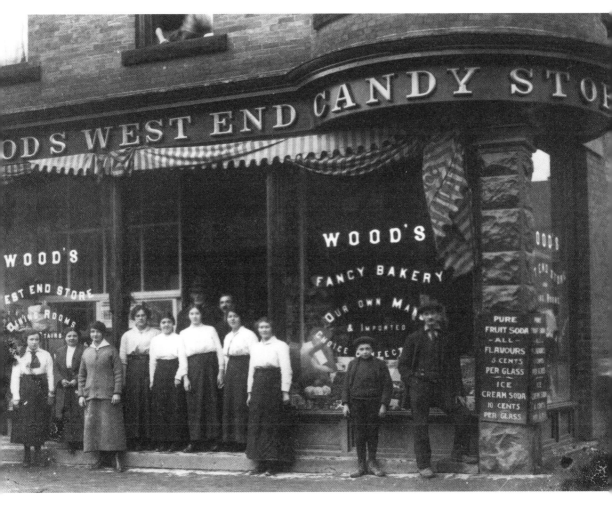

CHAPTER THREE

The 1910s

"By the 1910s, restaurants were on a fast track—decades of immigration had led to scores of new ways to dine."

If you chose to eat lunch in the dining car of *The Imperial* on your way from Montreal to Vancouver in 1912 via the Canadian Pacific Railway, you would have had a plethora of options for the midday à la carte: Chow Chow relishes, crabmeat cocktail, filet of halibut with sauté meunière, "red brand" sirloin steaks, creamed spinach, beet and egg salads, not to mention hot biscuits, Nestlé's Gruyère cheese, marmalade, fruit jelly with whipped cream and Fleischmann's yeast for 10 cents per brick.

By the 1910s, restaurants were on a fast track—decades of immigration had led to scores of new ways to dine. According to the 1911 census, more than half of the country's restaurant keepers were born outside Canada, and so were 78 percent of the men working at them as cooks, dishwashers and servers. In addition to a world war, labour movements and women's suffrage dominated the headlines during this period, and those who worked in restaurants demanded better pay and fewer hours; it was not a glamorous job.

Dining for the elite continued its devotion to the French kitchen, with languid multi-course meals of vichyssoise, lamb with mint sauce and roast duckling, all enjoyed by men in tuxedos and ladies in gowns as they sipped Champagne from crystal coupes. The slowly growing middle class ate simple three-course meals after a long hard day of work. And it got a little easier for women to go out to eat without the company of men—they dined in tearooms and restaurants near and around department stores. As more women entered the workforce, there were separate lunchrooms and restaurants for them. During the First World War, it became important for farmers to continue producing food for Britain and, afterward, a short depression caused an increase in food costs. In small towns, dining out was still an irregular occurrence, with people preferring the quality and quantity of eating at home, though on occasion they would grab a meal at the local hotel dining room.

Club Cafe

CALGARY, ALBERTA (1911–1946)

Club Cafe made theme restaurants cool before they were cool. Ron Beavers and his wife, Lina, of White Hill, Illinois, settled in Calgary in October 1911 after a nomadic career of exhibiting attractions on the carnival circuit across the Prairies. This showmanship would prove to be the key to their later success as restaurateurs and early promoters of the famed Calgary Stampede. In December 1911, they opened Club Cafe, which was both a lunch counter and a sit-down restaurant, at 111 8th Avenue East in downtown Calgary.

Ownership of cafes in the Prairies at the turn of the century was as transient as the rail workers (most didn't stay open for more than five years), but unlike many other restaurants during this time—established to service the rise of predominantly male urban office workers and rail workers—Club Cafe thrived because it also had a restaurant area with high-end decor and tuxedoed servers, for more leisurely eating. This combination became key to the success of one of the longest-running establishments in the city.

As a proud member of the Calgary Booster Club, Mr. Beavers jumped on the bandwagon (both literally and figuratively) when it came to promoting the Calgary Stampede, which started in 1912. Like many other Calgary restaurateurs, he decorated Club Cafe in a western theme every July and even changed the name to Roy's Chuck House (though he rarely changed the menu). On July 10, 1923, he went so far as to have pop culture cowboy Eddie King ride his horse through the restaurant, making the cover of the *Calgary Herald* that day.

In 1929, they added on the Spanish Room and the Club Cafe shifted to a more club-like scenario, offering up dishes like creamed oyster patties or jellied chicken sandwiches with a coffee for 40 cents, with live music after 8 p.m. Sadly, Club Cafe was destroyed by a fire in 1946, but its contribution to the dining scene in Calgary, and the fanfare surrounding the Stampede, lives on.

Cowboy on horse exiting from Club Cafe, Calgary, Alberta

Montreal Pool Room

MONTREAL, QUEBEC (1912–Present)

When Bulgarian immigrant Filipov Dakov got his start in the restaurant industry towing his chip wagon with a horse, he probably didn't imagine the little pool room he later opened in Montreal's redlight district would become a destination for food pilgrims in search of the beloved "steamie." A steamie—or *steamé*, as it's known in French—is a "Franglais" term that refers to how both the hot dog and the bun are steamed before being topped with mustard, chopped onion, relish and fresh cabbage slaw—never ketchup.

Dakov opened the Montreal Pool Room in 1912, and for decades the spot has fed those in search of a steamie after a night of drinking; everyone from Al Capone to Leonard Cohen are said to have downed a dog here. The pool tables themselves are long gone, and while some say that after the 1989 post-fire refurbishments it doesn't have the same grungy appeal, even a move across the street in 2010 couldn't stop patrons from coming. Ownership has changed hands many times; the latest owner is the Goulakos family, happy to land back on boulevard Saint-Laurent—their Greek ancestors ran a bar across the street for decades. There aren't many tables, just a few inside the narrow eatery, with a stainless-steel bar along one wall dotted with old Montreal maps and photographs. That's the Montreal Pool Room: seedy, dingy and iconic.

United Bakers Dairy

TORONTO, ONTARIO (1912–Present)

On any given morning in the past hundred years, one could hear Yiddish, Polish and English amid the clank of coffee cups and heavy white plates at United Bakers Dairy. The Ladovskys—Aaron and Sarah—both came from Kielce, Poland, but met in Toronto, where they fed the pillars of the Jewish community.

When they immigrated in the late 1910s, there were only three types of restaurants to open: a deli serving pastrami sandwiches, an appetizing store with bagels and lox, or a dairy restaurant. They chose the latter, starting with a bakery serving 5-cent coffees, and gave their customers a taste of home. Adam came from a family known for baking, and Sarah's Polish recipes kept the front door swinging, but they were also foundational to Toronto's Jewish community: Aaron was active in many unions, and people visited the restaurant for conversation, company or even in the hope of landing a job. It almost became a rite of passage for new immigrants to dine at the United Bakers Dairy.

As the city changed and the Jewish community of Toronto was pushed out of The Ward, so was the bakery from their three-storey brick building, moving onto Spadina Avenue with the rest of the community, before eventually landing in North York, but the relationship remained symbiotic. The dairy was as much the community itself as it was a place that the community cherished. In this, Toronto's oldest dairy restaurant, and one of the only ones left in North America, the menu hasn't changed too much since Aaron and Sarah first hung up their shingle in The Ward. The Greek salad added in the 1980s is a constant favourite, while the green split pea soup is beloved, and now there's mac and cheese and quinoa salad, but the latkes, kreplach and bagels remain at the heart of this family business. Today, Adam's great-grandson Nathan runs it, along with his parents and other family members.

Cheese Blintzes

Recipe from
United Bakers Dairy

The cheese blintzes are a customer favourite at United Bakers Dairy, and for good reason. Besides the fact that these cheesy crepes are hot, golden and delicious, they've been perfecting the recipe for more than 100 years. United Bakers uses dry 4% milk fat baker's cottage cheese from Western Creamery, but any pressed cottage cheese will do, and the cheese filling works well for kreplach too!

MAKES 10 BLINTZES

Pancakes

5 eggs

1 Tbsp (15 ml) vegetable oil

1 cup (250 ml) milk (preferably whole)

¾ cup (185 ml) all-purpose flour

Unsalted butter, for frying

FOR THE PANCAKES:

1. In a large bowl using a handheld mixer, beat together the eggs and oil until fluffy. Add the milk and beat until evenly blended. Gradually add the flour, beating out any lumps. Strain through a fine-mesh sieve set over a bowl. Refrigerate, covered, for up to 1 day if making ahead.

2. Lightly oil a 7-inch (8 cm) non-stick frying pan (or crepe pan, if you have one) and heat over medium-high heat. Lift the pan from the heat and ladle in ¼ cup (60 ml) of batter. Do this quickly as you tilt the pan in a circular motion so that the batter evenly covers the bottom of the pan. Quickly pour any excess batter back into the bowl. Return the pan to the heat and cook the pancake until brown at the edges—this should take between 45 and 60 seconds. Turn out the pancake onto a clean kitchen towel. Repeat until all the remaining batter has been used.

FOR THE FILLING:

3. In a medium bowl, break up the cottage cheese by hand or by beating with a rubber spatula. Add the egg yolks and sugar, and blend well. If not using immediately, transfer the filling to a bowl and refrigerate, covered, for up to 1 day.

4. Scoop ¼ cup (60 ml) of the filling onto the bottom third of a pancake, shaping it into a slender log. Fold the bottom of the pancake over the filling, fold in the sides, then roll to form a neat cylinder. Blintzes can be refrigerated, covered, for several hours or overnight.

TO SERVE:

5. Melt the butter in a large frying pan over medium heat. Fry the blintzes in batches, starting with the seam side down and turning once. Cook until the filling is heated through and the exterior is crisp and browned, about 3 minutes per side.

6. Serve immediately, with applesauce or sour cream, if desired.

Filling

1½ pounds (675 g) cottage cheese

4 large egg yolks

½ cup (125 ml) granulated sugar

To Serve

Applesauce or sour cream

Right: The last day at the Spadina location, in 1983
Left: The original location at 116 Agnes (Dundas), circa 1912

The Rex Hotel

WELLAND, ONTARIO (1915–Present)

A business by any other name has ice cream just as sweet. It was Bruno Carusetta who opened his ice cream shop, which turned into a pizza empire, and it's Bruno Carusetta who's running it today, more than a hundred years later. Three generations of Carusettas have successively taken what was once a small ice cream parlour on South Main Street, complete with wrought-iron tables and a marble soda fountain, and turned it into a restaurant, hotel and bar. When the restaurant opened, more than a thousand Italians were working on the Welland Canal (at least two dozen lost their lives during construction).

A SPECIALTY OF THE REX HOTEL LTD.

PIZZA SERVICE
```
Tomato Cheese.......................75¢
Tomato Cheese & Anchovies..........1.00
Tomato Cheese & Pepperoni.........1.00
Tomato  "  & Sweet Green Peppers..1.00
Tomato Cheese & Mushrooms.........1.00
Tomato Cheese & Green Olives......1.00
Tomato .Cheese & Fresh Sausage.....1.00
REX SPECIAL (With the works)......1.25
```

SERVED 5 p.m. to 12 p.m. DAILY

SATURDAYS 3 p.m. to 1 a.m.

Take out orders .10c Ex. PHONE RE. 4-4752

The family business has evolved and changed names several times since, shifting from The Tripoli (scooping ice cream) to The Napoli (serving pizza) in 1935, and then to The Marine during the Second World War, when the family changed the name to a more neutral term in an effort to stave off anti-Italian sentiments in Canada during the time (some locals referred to the theatre on King Street as the Garlic Opera because of its proximity to the Italian and Hungarian communities). Bruno Carusetta resigned from the local Italian chamber of commerce to avoid internment at the enemy alien camps enacted under the War Measures Act. Finally, the venue became The Rex Hotel, as it's known today, because the mayor called it so during the ribbon-cutting ceremony that very same day in 1948.

The Works pie is still the same: in 1963, the Rex Special was $1.25, and now $15 will get you the pizza, with pepperoni, mushrooms, green olives and sweet peppers. Ice cream sundaes are also still on the menu, and you can even get them deep-fried.

Bottom: The original ice cream parlour at The Tripoli

Green Lantern HALIFAX, NOVA SCOTIA (1917–1962)

The streetcar rumbled over cobblestoned Barrington Street as the women employed at William Hart's Green Lantern worked their way around the dining room. Miss Bella Bloom and Miss Elizabeth Heaton were just two of the dozen women who, in the late 1910s, worked at the busy teahouse and boarded across the city, as did Alfred Carter, who resided in Africville.

In 1917, Green Lantern quickly became the finest place to dine, with its 50-cent dinner consisting of soup (oxtail or cream of potato), followed by Baked Haddock à la Creole, then an entree choice of chicken croquette with cream sauce, baked sausage with bacon, or cold jellied corned beef, followed by cold tongue and boiled, browned mashed

Exterior of Green Lantern restaurant on Barrington Street, April 3, 1941

potatoes and string beans. Dessert was either fruit, rice custard pudding or a slice of pie (chosen from a selection of myriad flavours) with tea, coffee, hot chocolate or milk. Lunches were equally large: fresh halibut, steak and kidney pie, roast leg of veal and creamed carrots.

By the 1940s, the Green Lantern had morphed into a delicatessen with shelves for pastries, breads and confections. Later, mothers and daughters would stop by for a milkshake after a visit to Zellers down the street. Green Lantern was gone by the 1960s, but the restaurant's name stuck to the building as its most beloved tenant. In the 1970s, there were gay bars Club 777 and Thee Klub, and many of the Gay Alliance for Equality's first meetings were held there. In 2021, the renovated building became the Green Lantern condos.

The Only Seafood

VANCOUVER, BRITISH COLUMBIA (1917–2009)

From the very beginning, the 18 seats at The Only Seafood were hot. During the 1910s, East Hastings Street was the place to be. As the centre of Vancouver's downtown, it was home to all the best restaurants, theatres and bars. Nick Thodos came to Vancouver from Greece (via Yukon, chasing gold) and started cooking at the English Kitchen at 20 East Hastings in the early 1910s. Soon his brother Gustave joined him, and they bought the place. Five years later, the brothers moved five doors down, purchasing the Vancouver Oyster Saloon and the same year changing it to The Only.

Steamed, boiled and fried seafood was the name of the game. With Nick in the kitchen, they became known for their clams; his trick was to toss in some oregano, a Mediterranean twist he learned in Greece—the source for all his recipes and inspiration. The iconic neon sign went up in the 1950s and somehow withstood the City's 1960s bylaw that aimed to eliminate them for being trashy. Sadly, the neighbourhood declined, but the lineups at The Only never really did. In their heyday, they were serving upward of four hundred people a day with no refrigeration—even by the 1990s there were no fridges to keep the seafood cold, just the packed ice in the front window. That's how you know those clams were real fresh.

Balmoral Cafe

REGINA, SASKATCHEWAN (1918–1968)

The same year that Canadian women earned the right to vote, the waitresses at the newly opened Balmoral Cafe had had enough. They staged the first women's strike in Saskatchewan, demanding that their wages be brought up to $5 a week, their daily work hours be reduced from 15 to 10. The Regina labour council did little to help; the women went back to work without a raise.

By the 1920s, "Meet me at the Bal" was a common phrase among Reginians as the cafe, with its new soda fountain, birch mahogany booths, tile wainscoting and frescoes of mountains, flourished under the ownership of Nick Pappas and Albert Lallas, who had emigrated from Piraeus, Greece, in 1909. They were active members of the American Hellenic Educational Progressive Association, which aimed to protect the local Greek community from bigotry. The restaurants in the 1800 blocks of Scarth and Hamilton Streets in downtown Regina were mostly Greek-owned, and the area was known as "coffee rows." Here, diners would down 35-cent lunches of hot chicken sandwiches and coffee, or with toasted teacakes or flapper pie.

The cafe was open all hours and became a communal space for local sports teams and fans, where they balanced on the stools at the counter and demolished sizzling steaks.

Union Cafe

PONOKA, ALBERTA (1918–1953)

All the history books talk about the thousands of Chinese immigrants who came to Canada to build the railway, risking their lives for the sake of livelihood, but not many further illustrate what happened once the last spike was driven. Many former railway workers settled along the trans-Canadian railway route and helped establish those small towns, opening stores, laundries and restaurants.

James Mah Poy came to Canada in 1902, opened a laundry in Ponoka, Alberta, in 1906, bringing his wife, Liang Shi, over in 1912. Together they opened the Union Cafe in 1918 and grew their family, becoming pillars in the community. The cafe always stayed open late to accommodate train travellers—it's said that James sometimes would be waiting at the station with a pot of hot coffee for those dozily disembarking from the 3 a.m. Calgary–Edmonton run.

Hong Mah Poy, Toy Win Chun and James Mah Poy in front of Union Cafe, Ponoka, Alberta

Hoito

THUNDER BAY, ONTARIO (1918–2020)

Pancakes for the people by the people. The bright blue of the restaurant sign blares from beneath the Finlandia Club in Thunder Bay, which was originally the Finnish Labour Temple. Hoito was a favourite place to eat in Thunder Bay for more than a century. *Hoito* translates to "care" in Finnish, and the love the residents

of Thunder Bay have for this institution is fierce—and so was Hoito's care in the making of their world-famous pancakes.

The co-op was founded on May 1, 1918, amid the War Measures Act, halted immigration and a changing political climate, when 59 people pooled their money together, contributing $5 each. It was spearheaded by A.T. Hill, who became the first restaurant manager (he later founded the Communist Party of Canada, and spent some time in prison in the 1930s). With the co-operative founded, local Finns could eat as much as they wanted at Hoito for $6, and even by the 1970s, when the co-op evolved into the Finlandia Association of Thunder Bay, the club charged only $1 for each dinner, keeping meals accessible to many. The co-op owned the restaurant up until its closure. (In my mind, I can still hear the screech of the metal chairs on the concrete floor, and see those long communal tables and blond wood walls that haven't been updated in generations.)

At its peak, Hoito fed hundreds of people a day. After years of financial struggles, the restaurant closed for good in 2020, when you could still get three plate-sized pancakes for less than $10 ($9.50, to be exact).

Finnish Pancakes

Recipe inspired by
Hoito

In true Finnish fashion, these plate-sized thin pancakes are on the savoury side, so they're incredibly versatile. You can eat them with a side of scrambled eggs and bacon just as easily as you can with whipped cream and strawberries, or topped with apple pie filling, like how they used to serve them at Hoito.

MAKES 6 PANCAKES

5 eggs

6 cups (1.5 L) whole milk

¼ cup (60 ml) granulated sugar

2 tsp (10 ml) salt

3 cups (750 ml) all-purpose flour

Butter or margarine, for frying

1. Whisk together the eggs, milk, sugar and salt.

2. Slowly add the flour, stirring continuously, until just combined. Take care not to overmix.

3. Melt some butter in a preheated griddle or large non-stick frying pan over medium heat until it bubbles.

4. Ladle in a scoop of the batter to make a large, thin pancake, tilting the pan to spread the batter evenly.

5. Fry until golden on the bottom, flipping once bubbles begin to appear in the middle, about 2 minutes. Cook for another 2 minutes, until golden on the second side. Serve immediately.

Opposite: Finnish Labour Temple circa 1940
Left: Hoito Co-operative Restaurant cheque, December 18, 1939 cheque no. 561

Mel's Tea Room

SACKVILLE, NEW BRUNSWICK (1919–2022)

When Melbourne Goodwin opened his ice cream and fruit parlour in 1919, he no doubt was aware that Mount Allison University was a five-minute walk down the road. For more than one hundred years, students have squished into these small wooden booths, first for egg creams, ginger ales and ice cream sundaes at what was originally known as Goodwin's. Three decades later the parlour shifted gears, transforming into Mel's Tea Room when it moved two doors down. In 1944, it lit up the neon sign it's now known for and started up the flattop for the burgers and milkshakes that drew patrons for almost 80 years. Mel's closed in 2022 and was put on the market, its future unknown.

The Arbor

PORT DOVER, ONTARIO (1919–Present)

The hot dog stand on the corner of Walker and Main Streets really is a cornerstone of Port Dover. When the restaurant reopens for the season, it's a sure sign to the community that summer is on the horizon, and that horizon is ablaze with the Golden Glow, a freshly squeezed citrus drink that The Arbor is famous for. The corner stand was first opened by George Holden in 1912, but it was Carl Ryerse who, having taken over after a string of owners in 1919, came up with the golden ticket: the Golden Glow. He patented the beverage in 1929 and didn't share the recipe with anyone but his sons; it's said that the staff would juice 144 oranges and then he would go into the back room to make it.

Droves of sun-seekers flock to the area every summer to soak up the Lake Erie vibe, and a must-stop for many is The Arbor, for hot dogs, hamburgers and dipped ice cream. A speciality created by Ryerse, The Arbor's dipped ice creams were actual bricks of homemade ice cream cut into eight portions and then placed on a stick, dipped in chocolate and rolled in cashews. And the secret ingredient in the Golden Glow? A well-kept trade secret to this very day.

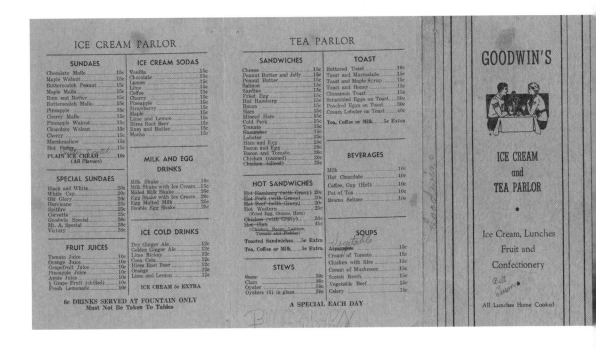

ICE CREAM PARLOR

SUNDAES
Chocolate Mallo	15c
Maple Walnut	15c
Butterscotch Peanut	15c
Maple Mallo	15c
Rum and Butter	15c
Butterscotch Mallo	15c
Pineapple	15c
Cherry Mallo	15c
Pineapple Walnut	15c
Chocolate Walnut	15c
Cherry	15c
Marshmallow	15c
Hot Fudge	15c
PLAIN ICE CREAM	10c
(All Flavors)	

SPECIAL SUNDAES
Black and White	20c
White Cap	20c
Old Glory	20c
Hurricane	25c
Spitfire	25c
Corvette	25c
Goodwin Special	30c
Mt. A. Special	30c
Victory	30c

FRUIT JUICES
Tomato Juice	10c
Orange Juice	10c
Grapefruit Juice	10c
Pineapple Juice	10c
Apple Juice	10c
½ Grape Fruit (chilled)	10c
Fresh Lemonade	10c

ICE CREAM SODAS
Vanilla	15c
Chocolate	15c
Lemon	15c
Lime	15c
Coffee	15c
Cherry	15c
Pineapple	15c
Strawberry	15c
Maple	15c
Lime and Lemon	15c
Hires Root Beer	15c
Rum and Butter	15c
Mocha	15c

MILK AND EGG DRINKS
Milk Shake	10c
Milk Shake with Ice Cream	15c
Maled Milk Shake	20c
Egg Shake with Ice Cream	20c
Egg Malted Milk	25c
Double Egg Shake	25c

ICE COLD DRINKS
Dry Ginger Ale	12c
Golden Ginger Ale	12c
Lime Rickey	12c
Coca Cola	12c
Hires Root Beer	12c
Orange	12c
Lime and Lemon	12c
ICE CREAM 5c EXTRA	

6c DRINKS SERVED AT FOUNTAIN ONLY
Must Not Be Taken To Tables

TEA PARLOR

SANDWICHES
Cheese	15c
Peanut Butter and Jelly	15c
Peanut Butter	15c
Salmon	15c
Sardine	15c
Fried Egg	15c
Hot Hamburg	15c
Bacon	15c
Ham	15c
Minced Ham	15c
Cold Pork	15c
Tomato	15c
Cucumber	15c
Lobster	20c
Ham and Egg	20c
Bacon and Egg	20c
Bacon and Tomato	20c
Chicken (canned)	20c
Chicken (sliced)	25c

HOT SANDWICHES
Hot Hamburg (with Gravy)	20c
Hot Pork (with Gravy)	20c
Hot Beef (with Gravy)	20c
Hot Western	25c
(Fried Egg, Onions, Ham)	
Chicken (with Gravy)	30c
Hot Club	45c
(Chicken, Bacon, Lettuce, Tomato and Pickles)	
Toasted Sandwiches	5c Extra
Tea, Coffee or Milk	5c Extra

STEWS
Corn	30c
Clam	30c
Oyster	50c
Oysters (6) in glass	30c

A SPECIAL EACH DAY

TOAST
Buttered Toast	10c
Toast and Marmalade	15c
Toast and Maple Syrup	15c
Toast and Honey	15c
Cinnamon Toast	15c
Scrambled Eggs on Toast	30c
Poached Eggs on Toast	30c
Cream Lobster on Toast	40c
Tea, Coffee or Milk	5c Extra

BEVERAGES
Milk	10c
Hot Chocolate	10c
Coffee, Cup (Hot)	10c
Pot of Tea	10c
Bromo Seltzer	10c

SOUPS
Asparagus	15c
Cream of Tomato	15c
Chicken with Rice	15c
Cream of Mushroom	15c
Scotch Broth	15c
Vegetable Beef	15c
Celery	15c

GOODWIN'S

ICE CREAM and TEA PARLOR

Ice Cream, Lunches
Fruit and
Confectionery

All Lunches Home Cooked

Top: Menu from Goodwin's Ice Cream
and Tea Parlor, 1940s
Bottom left: Group of female students sitting
in a booth at Goodwin's restaurant (Mel's), 1941
Bottom right: Arbor exterior with staff, 1936

CHAPTER FOUR

The 1920s

"The lunch counter provided urbanites with a convenient way to enjoy the midday meal."

When broadcaster and homemaking instructor Kate Aitken took over the Balcony Restaurant in the Women's Building at the Canadian National Exhibition—aka the Ex—in Toronto in 1926, she took special care to showcase food from each province, prepared for the daily luncheon provided by the Department of Agriculture: Alberta eggs, canned meats and pickled vegetables were showcased, as were BC flowers adorning the tables; jellies made from West Coast cherries and Quebec cheeses followed maple syrup demonstrations. The Balcony Restaurant employed mostly women (and high-school home economics students), who were paid double the going rate. And when Aitken, who was well on her way to being known as Mrs. A across the country, took over the Women's World Tea Room, and the Tea Room in Teen Town in the 1940s, she used the restaurants as a place to teach women how to properly host a dinner, but also a way to advertise new kitchen appliances to the Ex's visitors.

The post–First World War influx of Jewish immigrants from Eastern Europe saw an explosion of kosher delis across the country, and the lunch counter provided urbanites with a convenient way to enjoy the midday meal, and shifted the main meal of the day from lunch to supper—people opted for quick and easy meals on the go during the day, settling in at home for larger meals in the evening. And yet, more people than ever before were eating out as the restaurant industry became more standardized and offered more variety in restaurant types. Transportation in major cities improved too, allowing more women to enter the workforce and commute via public transit. The Chinese Exclusion Act, which banned the immigration of most Chinese people to Canada, came into effect in 1923, in addition to other legislation that forbade white women from working in Chinese-owned restaurants. Meanwhile, people from certain parts of Europe were on the not-preferred list. International demand for Canadian raw materials rose, and increased profits in the wheat, mining, forestry, hydropower and oil sectors led to a new level of wealth across the country. The Ontario Restaurant Association was founded in 1928 with a focus on modern industrial life, promising a bountiful future for restaurants, as did the Canadian Restaurant Association, established the same year.

Johnson's Cafe

EDMONTON, ALBERTA (1920–1961)

"Meet me under the clock at Johnson's" became a common catchphrase in Edmonton throughout the 1920s. Underneath that large Shamrock Pure Meats clock at the corner of Jasper Avenue and 101st Street was Johnson's Cafe, a landmark eatery and meeting place in Edmonton as the city gradually became the "gateway to the North." Located inside the Hotel Selkirk, it was one of many coffee shops where people could pause for a break from shopping or their daily errands. Greek immigrant Constantinos Yeanitchous, who changed his name to Con Johnson because most people couldn't pronounce his birthname, set out white tablecloths for patrons of the cafe, on the main floor of the hotel until it was destroyed by fire in 1961. Today, you can visit the cafe's replica at Fort Edmonton Park on 1920 Street and choose from an updated menu of dishes made with Alberta produce.

Érablière Meunier & Fils

RICHELIEU, QUEBEC (1920–Present)

Dining out is often all about timing, but when it comes to meals during the sugaring-off season, scheduling is on a whole other level. Canada produces 80 percent of the world's maple syrup supply, and most of that is made in Quebec. The sugaring-off season there is in the springtime, when the nights are still cold but the days are filled with warm sunshine—usually from early March until the end of April. It brings hundreds of thousands of Québécois into the forests to dine at the numerous sugar shack restaurants across the province.

"Les cabanes à sucre" or sugar shacks have a long history, dating back to the 17th century, when settlers learned from the Indigenous peoples how to tap trees. These days, some two hundred shacks are equipped with spaces for tour buses bringing the hungry hoards. Érablière Meunier & Fils has been sugaring trees since the 1920s and offering up the sugar shack experience for decades. Long tables clad in red plaid are laden with classic sugar shack meals, starting with pea soup, followed by a banquet of maple ham, baked beans, oreilles de crisse, omelettes and tourtière.

Exterior of Johnson's Cafe at the Selkirk Hotel

Famous for
SPANISH DISHES

SID BEECH'S TAMALE PARLOR
Menu

"A Little Bit of Mexico"

GENERAL PRINTING
H-1004 55-12

Sid Beech's

TAMALE PARLOR
615 ROBSON ST.
VANCOUVER
CANADA

28 YEARS IN SAME LOCATION

M E N U

Try it!

GIANT WEINERS
with Chile and Beans .... .60

MENU

m-'m Good

SPANISH CHICKEN
with Fried Rice, Bread, Butter & Coffee 1.00

COLD CHICKEN *with Tomatoes* .... .85

Tamales

Special Chicken Tamale	.45
Chicken Tamale, smothered with Chile	.65
Chicken Tamale, smothered with Italian Cheese	.55
Huskless Tamale	.45
Texas Tamale, smothered with Chili	.55
Texas Tamale	.40
Chicken Tamale, smothered with Chili and Cheese	.75
Texas Tamale, smothered with Chili and Cheese	.65
Tamales Con Queso	.80

Enchiladas

Enchiladas Con Queso (Corn Tortilla)	.60
Special Enchilada (Egg Tortilla)	.75
Side Order Grated Italian Cheese	.20

Chili

Chili Con Carne, with Beans	.30
Fried Eggs, Con Chili	.50
Chili Con Carne, with Rice	.50
Order Plain Beans	.15
Hot Chili Sandwich	.40

Ice Cream

Vanilla Ice Cream	.10

Pies and Cakes

Assorted Pies, per cut	.10
Fruit Cake, per order	.10
Cookies, per order	.10

Beverages

Coffee	.10
Pot of Tea	.10
Milk	.10
Buttermilk	.10
Chocolate	.10
Tomato Juice	.15

Soups

Cream of Tomato Soup	.15

Noodles

Chinese Noodles, Plain	.35
With Eggs	.45
Bowl of Rice	.15
Bowl of Rice with Cream	.20
Noodles Con Chili	.50
No Half Order Noodles Served.	

Ravioli

Ravioli	.55
Ravioli and Spaghetti	.70

Cocktails

Crab Cocktail	.35
Shrimp Cocktail	.35
Oyster Cocktail	.35

Sandwiches

Fried Ham	.30
Denver	.45
Chicken	.45
Fried Egg	.20
Cheese	.20

Sid Beech's Tamale Parlor

VANCOUVER, BRITISH COLUMBIA (1922–1955)

Two years after Sid Beech's Tamale Parlour opened on Robson Street, the *Vancouver Sun*'s famed fictional columnist Edith Adams wrote about the restaurant's Mexican cuisine in a 1924 column, saying: "One of the marks of a true Bohemian in Vancouver is an occasional visit, preferable after 10 p.m., to the Vancouver Tamale Parlor, 605 Robson Street, where hotly spiced Mexican food in the way of hot tamales, enchiladas, chilli con carne, and spaghetti con chilli may be had."

Sid Beech wasn't Mexican, however; he was born in Clapham, England, in 1891 and immigrated to Winnipeg with his parents at age 14. After sustaining a serious injury in France during the First World War, he spent some time in Seattle learning from a friend how to make Mexican food. His tamales became a fan favourite at Sid Beech's during the three decades of the restaurant's operation, in the illustrious Orillia building. The menu focused on Mexican and Spanish cuisine but did have a variety of other dishes, like Chinese noodles with eggs, ravioli and spaghetti (together in one dish) and spaghetti con chili, not to mention sandwiches and Dewar's dry ginger ale by the pint. The Special Chicken Tamales smothered in chili and carefully wrapped in corn husks imported from Los Angeles—which in the 1940s would have cost those bohemian diners 40 cents—were so beloved some patrons ordered them by mail. Others loved Sid's tamale sauce so much they had it flown to their homes—by the 1950s, big milk jugs filled with the sauce were landing on doorsteps across the province.

Left: Menu of Sid Beech's Tamale Parlour circa 1948-1952

Carriage Room, Glynmill Inn

CORNER BROOK, NEWFOUNDLAND AND LABRADOR
(1924–Present)

Within a year of opening, the Carriage Room at the Glynmill Inn was the place to dine in Corner Brook. On New Year's Eve 1925, two hundred revellers rang in the new year with whistles and squeakers in the dining room "decorated with twisted rope festoons of dark green and scarlet, hung with red balls of various sizes, while about the electric fixtures and over the doorways bunches of evergreens were cluttered."

The hotel quickly became a luxury destination for American and Canadian tourists eager to see the pine-clad hills of Newfoundland's western coast. What started as executive housing for a pulp and paper mill (eventually, the world's largest) became, in the early 1920s, a Corner Brook landmark. After a day of fishing on the Humber River, guests would dine at the Carriage Room, with its large windows, starched white tablecloths and silver service, feasting on boiled Newfoundland salmon with parsley sauce, roast spring lamb with gravy, and Yankee roast potatoes, and finishing with pistachio ice cream.

Almost one hundred years later, the Carriage Room is still one of the best places in town to eat. They still serve up salmon on white tablecloths, but with contemporary additions, like avocado salad and dill vinaigrette.

Georgian Room at Eaton's

TORONTO, ONTARIO (1924–1976)

Society saw the term "ladies who lunch" enter the vernacular in the 1920s, and in Canada, that was all because of Lady Eaton and her chicken pot pie. Flora McCrea Eaton married John Eaton, the son of Irish immigrant and department-store magnate Timothy Eaton, in 1901 and helped redefine restaurant dining in Canada. Eaton's department stores were the first in Canada to have electric lights, telephones, escalators and elevators. This desire to be at the cutting-edge helped cement the tradition of ladies who lunch.

Georgian Room, 1924

After the death of her husband in 1922 (her father-in-law had died in 1907), Lady Eaton found her moment to establish a state-of-the-art restaurant. The crowning achievement of her dining-out dynasty was the Georgian Room at the flagship Queen Street store in Toronto. Lady Eaton was an avid traveller, and her dining out in New York and London had prepared her to create the most modern of restaurants. From the architecture to the menu, the Georgian Room had the best of everything when it opened on October 10, 1924. It cost $50,868 ($811,633.46 in present-day dollars) to outfit the restaurant with tableware, including china designed by Thomas Haviland, and Lady Eaton herself chose the Chinese silks adorning the walls.

The effort was worth it, as the Georgian Room is said to have revolutionized restaurant service the world over. Dishes like Cheese Dreams (think of it like a grilled cheese and Welsh rarebit had a baby), and Queen Elizabeth cake filled the menu and helped shape "Canadian" cuisine, but it was the chicken pot pie, not the chandeliers nor white tablecloths, that rings eternal in the nostalgic memory of those who ate there. A bubbly mess of moist chicken, red pimento, potato balls and butter underneath a phalanx of pastry, crispy from the egg-and-milk glaze, it has earned its rightful place in Canadian culinary history.

Tomahawk Restaurant

NORTH VANCOUVER, BRITISH COLUMBIA (1926–Present)

Some might look at the totem poles outside the low-rise brick building in North Vancouver and think the place is some odd unauthorized museum of Indigenous art, and the Tomahawk, one of the city's oldest eateries, does have a special relationship with Indigenous artists. Chick Chamberlain got his start in the restaurant industry by opening a small coffee shop and rental cottages with his brother in the early 1920s, where he cut his teeth cooking. He opened Tomahawk Restaurant in 1926 and, after a short stint as a drive-in restaurant didn't prove successful due to a lot of dust and a lack of cars, the restaurant became a fixture in the community.

During the Depression years, those who sidled up to the 14 seats around the horseshoe bar enclosing the grill and couldn't pay the bill would offer up masks, pots and paintings in exchange for their meal. Those 14 stools still stand chromed and tall at the bar today, as does the eclectic collection of First Nations art that on its own brings diners to the Tomahawk, in particular the painting of Chief Simon Baker and carvings by Squamish artist Robert Yelton.

These days, Chick's son Chuck runs the place, and views his family as stewards of the Indigenous ephemera that crowd every surface of the restaurant. Well into his 80s, Chuck still opens the doors at 7 a.m., with a hot pot of coffee at the ready to wash down those huge breakfasts, and later in the day, cooks charbroiled burgers named after famous Indigenous leaders.

Schwartz's

MONTREAL, QUEBEC (1928–Present)

When you finally make it inside Schwartz's after braving the inevitable lineup down Saint-Laurent partially sheltered by the Montreal Hebrew Delicatessen sign, it's not much to look at: a tired drop ceiling with whitish walls lined with old pictures and furnished with chrome tables and chairs, and stools lining the counter. But this place has reached pilgrimage status when it comes to Canadian food, specifically Quebec cuisine. Its Montreal smoked-meat sandwich—layers upon layers of smoked beef (the recipe has a Romanian and Turkish lineage) piled high onto rye bread and garnished with little other than mustard—is a bucket-list food item when in Montreal.

But the Jewish deli that pumps out pastrami's cousin by the pound wasn't the first restaurant deli in Montreal. It was preceded by the British-American Delicatessen Store in 1909, then Bens Delicatessen shortly after, and when the Montreal Hebrew Delicatessen (Schwartz's official name) was opened in 1928, it was more of a takeaway situation for Romanian Jews who filled the Plateau neighbourhood. Owner Reuben Schwartz sold his 13-cent sandwiches to hordes of hungry people and is credited with popularizing the Montreal smoked-meat sandwich, which is now one of the most recognizable Canadian dishes.

The Montreal Smoked Meat Sandwich at Schwartz's

White Spot

VANCOUVER, BRITISH COLUMBIA (1928–Present)

On the 10th anniversary of White Spot Barbecue, restaurateur and former Minnesotan Nat Bailey thanked Vancouver's motorists for making his business a success. And he does have the automobile to thank for that. He started his business by remodelling a Model T into a food truck, then selling hot dogs for 10 cents and ice cream for 5 cents at Vancouver's lookout points.

The first White Spot drive-in restaurant opened in June 1928 in a small white log cabin at Granville and 67th Streets, serving up fried chicken, milkshakes and the now-famous Triple O burger. Ten years later, a new dining room opened on the very same spot with murals on the walls depicting buffalo and bucolic scenes, and large knotty pine booths where staff served up special chicken and steak dinners, meatloaf and blueberry pie. Today, there are more than a hundred locations of the family-favourite restaurant in British Columbia and Alberta, along with Triple O's, the offshoot burger joint that took off in the late 1990s and expanded into Asia.

Top: White Spot dining room,
June 1945
Bottom: A White Spot server, 1950

Skinner's

LOCKPORT, MANITOBA (1929–Present)

In the 1920s, the only way to get to Selkirk from Winnipeg was along River Road. So, when James Skinner decided he wanted to open a restaurant but was denied land in Selkirk by the town council, he wound up at Lockport, a popular destination for Winnipeggers looking to escape the heat of the city, and to boat and fish on the Red River, made deep by the locks there. The former grocery store owner opened Skinner's in 1929 as a tearoom serving light lunches, with a takeout window for ice creams and hot dogs. Despite it being the Depression, he pushed on, and eventually owned a city block, with several kitchens employing dozens of people.

Today, Skinner's Hwy 44 is owned by the Thompson family, who took over in 1979 (the Skinners sold in 1972) and serves single, double and triple hot dogs, along with burgers and fries, chicken fingers and tall milkshakes.

The Senator

TORONTO, ONTARIO (1929–Present)

Toronto's oldest diner sits on Victoria Street, wedged between a jazz bar and a parking lot, in a building constructed in the 1850s by the Salvation Army. Its first iteration was as the Busy Bee Diner, opened by a Macedonian man named Robert Angeloff in 1929. As a lunch counter and late-night spot, it serviced those who worked in the area or were seeing a vaudeville show—Victoria Street was in the heart of early-20th-century Toronto's theatre district. One long counter with chrome seats, espresso-coloured wall panelling and small booths with coat hooks welcomed those looking for hot coffee and sandwiches.

As the city shifted around it, The Senator changed hands between Macedonian and Bulgarian ownership several times: In 1948, George Nicolau bought the diner, renovating it with the help of the Toronto Refrigeration Company and transforming it into the beloved Senator it is today, complete with red leather banquettes. The father of Canadian filmmaker Ted Kotcheff, a Bulgarian immigrant whose name was changed from Tsotcheff to Kotcheff because the immigration officer couldn't read Cyrillic, ran the place, among others, during the 1950s, then passed it on to son Nick and nephew Cecil Djambazis in the 1960s.

The Senator remained closed throughout most of the COVID-19 pandemic, but after 884 days, owner Robert Sniderman (who has run the place with baker and now GM Anne Hollyer for almost 40 years) reopened in the fall of 2022.

The interior of The Senator

Tea house where meals were first served at Sooke Harbour House circa 1937

Sooke Harbour House

SOOKE, BRITISH COLUMBIA (1929–Present)

The site of Sooke Harbour House, overlooking Sooke Basin, has always been about local food. What started as a seasonal camping and fishing ground of the T'Sou-ke First Nation became a modest tearoom in the 1920s when Czechoslovakian immigrant Anthony Kohout purchased the property, building a small restaurant and hotel. Even back in the 1930s and '40s, the community knew how special the place was: ads in the *Victoria Times Colonist* stated that it offered "scenic beauty, good food and a perfect place to rest and recuperate."

In 1979, Frederique and Sinclair Philip bought the place and expanded the guestrooms and dining experience. As innkeepers, the Philips transformed it from a quaint but run-down inn into a must-visit culinary crusade for Slow Food enthusiasts. Pacific Sashimi was served with T'Sou-ke–grown fresh wasabi from down the road, Dungeness crab from the inlet and the chanterelles foraged in the forest nearby. Their influence on the Slow Food movement and their close work with Vancouver Island's producers and fishers were recognized with the first-ever Governor General's Award in Celebration of the Nation's Table (Mentorship and Inspiration) in 2010.

Sadly, the couple who made Slow Food cool have been involved in an excruciatingly sluggish lawsuit after attempting to sell the property in 2014 to Timothy Durkin and Roger Gregory of SHH Holdings. In 2020, IAG Developments purchased the property, promising a renovation and a reopen, which at time of writing had yet to occur.

CHAPTER FIVE

The 1930s

"The worldwide depression of the 1930s had a major impact on where Canada ate."

An unnamed man under the moniker "Tired and Hungry" wrote a letter to the editor of the *Vancouver Sun*, published in the September 29, 1931, issue. The diatribe described the paltry restaurant dinner he was given on a government relief meal ticket as "one spoonful of potatoes, two pieces of beef as big as the end of my thumb, about six pieces (small cubes) of carrots and gravy. Bread, a small piece of butter, and coffee milk or tea," and complained that a non-relief meal for the same price would offer much more value. While restaurant relief tickets were used heavily in Vancouver and other major cities in Canada, often to feed single, unemployed men, the programs were riddled with profiteering, racism against non-white restaurant owners and overvaluing of poor-quality meals.

The worldwide depression of the 1930s had a major impact on where Canada ate. Thousands unemployed (one in nine Canadians was on some form of government assistance), drought in the Prairies, low wheat prices, plagues of grasshoppers, and hailstorms all affected the restaurant industry, but because the country had become so urban, there were enough people who still needed to eat in restaurants, and though sales did decline throughout the decade, the number of restaurants actually increased.

In the restaurant industry, there was a big emphasis on standardization, efficiency and cleanliness, along with the introduction of refrigeration even for the smallest of cafes. And those small cafes became community spaces and boarding houses for immigrants and their families. More than 30 percent of Canada's workforce was out of a job by 1933, and those who did work in restaurants, most often immigrants, were paid poorly and worked many hours just to make ends meet. Enter the Food Workers Industrial Union, an offshoot of Workers Unity League, which, with 21 locals across the country by 1934, fought for improved conditions for food workers.

Gem Cafe

SASKATOON, SASKATCHEWAN (1931–1971)

In the 1930s, the Greek community was just getting started in downtown Saskatoon, but almost all the restaurants on Second Avenue South were owned by Greeks. In fact, the major founding families, the Girgulises, Chroneses, Geatroses and Pontikes, all were from the village of Kastri, though they arrived in different ways and at different times. Jim Chrones emigrated from Greece in 1913 but didn't end up in Saskatoon until 1929, opening the Gem Cafe at 213 Second Avenue South two years later, where it became an institution, along with other Greek-owned restaurants who were part of the secret-not-so-secret Big Seven Group, like the Elite Cafe owned by the "Uncle Bill" Girgulis and his brothers.

Chrones was always improving the restaurant with renovations and updates, and taking out big spreads in the newspaper to tell everyone about it. For the February 1939 grand reopening, the *StarPhoenix* wrote about the 24 red leather stools surrounding a black-and-red three-sided counter finished in a "new way" with lights of various colours, walls with five shades going from white to tan, white-and-red glass chandeliers and the 15 booths in the dining room—"they are cream coloured and the lights are set in silver-coloured fixtures. Each booth has a mirror." Chrones's family legacy is one of the great places to eat. Never mind that The Gem Cafe was the first restaurant in the city to serve liquor.

The lunch counter at the Gem Cafe after their 1947 remodel

Salisbury House

WINNIPEG, MANITOBA (1931–Present)

Established in a little A-frame on Fort Street, Salisbury House started off with "dine for a dime": you could get a coffee, made with a fancy new Silex machine, for five cents and a hamburger for another nickel. When Salisbury House first opened, founder Roger Erwin decided he didn't want to sell hamburgers; he didn't like the name of this new American food, so he called it a "nip." This nickname came from the patty being a nip, or small portion, of Salisbury steak, which was then topped with grilled onions and served on a soft homemade bun—or, as Erwin called it, a "steak delicacy on a bun." The first location did well immediately.

When Erwin opened the second location at 254 Kennedy Street in 1932, *The Winnipeg Tribune* reported that it was "a peculiar little building with a high-pitched roof, that from its appearance, might have been picked up in an English village of a century ago and dropped down in its present location." Well, that little pitched roof, painted bright red with leftover barn paint, became an emblem and a beacon to hungry nip-searchers for generations. "Look for the little red roof" became Sals' slogan, and when it became a 24-hour eatery, it also became a late-night favourite for Manitobans. Now with more than 15 locations, whether you're having a quick Nip at the airport or sitting down for a full-service dining experience (including their famous red velvet cake for dessert), the nostalgia factor reaches its peak, just like that little red roof.

Old Spain

CHARLOTTETOWN, PRINCE EDWARD ISLAND (1932–1975)

When the Old Spain was very new, it was a tearoom and restaurant proudly decorated in a Spanish style. Brightly coloured walls and archways, furnishings from Holman's department store, and romantic accents were selected by Milton Bell and business partner Harry Richardson to give the Kent Street restaurant a European flair upon its opening in December 1932. It was Rita Bell, Milton's wife, who headed up the confectionery side of things, offering an assortment of sweets, candies and fruits, along with hot fountain drinks like hot fudges, hot lemonades and hot egg drinks.

While the decor of the Old Spain skewed Romanesque, the food was a snapshot of Prince Edward Island in the 1930s. On Sundays, a special stuffed roast chicken and roast goose dinner was served, as well as dainty lunches for afternoon tea and lengthy bridge games for the ladies. Perfection-brand ice cream was on offer on the daily and those wanting to know the future could have their tea leaves read by Mrs. Brewster from 4 to 9 p.m.

Later, the Old Spain became a local favourite during the Second World War, frequented by Royal Air Force servicemen stationed at the RCAF Station Charlottetown (now the airport) as part of the British Commonwealth Air Training Plan, no doubt mingling with Prince of Wales College students. In the 1960s, it became an even more happening hot spot when it opened The Granada upstairs, and through the 1990s hosted a myriad of music acts. By 2001 the series of rooms cobbled together were know as the biggest bar in eastern Canada. The building's peaked roof is still a local landmark today, though the Old Spain is but a memory—Hopyard Beer Bar is now in its place.

Green Door

VANCOUVER, BRITISH COLUMBIA (1935–1999)

Strolling down Market Alley, behind the 100 block of East Pender Street, in the 1930s, one would see an array of coloured doors—one orange, one red, and one green—each leading to a Chinese restaurant: Vancouver's Chinatown had become a tourist destination catering to white tourists. Indeed, by the 1930s, there were chop suey houses across the country. In fact, the 1931 census reports that about 20 percent of restaurants in Canada belonged to owners of Chinese origin, when at the time Chinese people represented only 1 percent of the population—the restaurant industry, like laundry service, was one of few commercial enterprises from which Chinese were not racially excluded.

The Green Door restaurant opened in 1935 in the back of 111 East Pender, a building constructed in 1903 by Chu Lai that was initially the private kitchen for the West Coast Fisherman's Club. In Vancouver's 1930s Chinatown, it was typical for a building to have a trading company on the street level and residential rooms or private gambling clubs upstairs. An open kitchen with a huge

Green Door, October 3, 1977

chopping block looked onto a dining room with six green stools saddled up to a green counter.

By the 1960s, Market Alley had reached mythic status, its restaurants feeding bohemians and students alike. Some said there was even a giant pot of communal rice in the middle of the room at the Green Door. Chinatown boomeranged back into being a drug-fuelled area in the 1980s and 1990s, and when the Green Door closed in 1999, owner Wallace Chan blamed drugs for its end.

Java Shop

FORT MACLEOD, ALBERTA (1935–2008)

For some, the Java Shop is where Ennis eats a slice of pie, in the Oscar-winning film *Brokeback Mountain*, but for the citizens of Fort Macleod, it was first and foremost their community meeting place. Located on the corner of Second Avenue and 23rd Street, it was open 24 hours a day, a hub of Fort Macleod, which is itself considered the crossroads of Alberta and, in the late 19th century, was a base for the RCMP.

Albert Swinarton and Hugh Craig opened the Java Shop in the summer of 1935 before moving it into the then new Greyhound bus terminal in 1939 as a full-service cafe with complete meals, quick lunches, coffee, ice cream, soft drinks and even tobacco. Patrons frequented the Java Shop as part of their daily ritual, or stopped in for the morning coffee or a bite of lunch when picking up Christmas packages or loved ones delivered to the station by Greyhound. It was also loved by the bus drivers, who could expect a satisfying hot meal any time of day. It was such an institution that, in 2017, the Elk Point Community Choir put on a play by Roger Cosgrove titled *A Day at the Java Shop & Greyhound Bus Depot*.

Le Salad Bar

MONTREAL, QUEBEC (1935–1945)

"Get your vitamins at the Salad Bar," said the 1943 *Gazette* ad. The *grand-mère* of French cooking in Quebec was never Julia Child, it was Jehane Benoît, and she was very concerned that you weren't getting enough veggies. By the age of 21, the Montrealer had studied at both the Cordon Bleu and the Sorbonne in Paris in the 1920s. In 1935, she opened her first restaurant, Le Salad Bar at 1324 Sherbrooke Street West in Montreal.

Outside of a small sect of turn-of-the-century restaurants that focused on nut meat, like the Apple Tree in Winnipeg, Le Salad Bar was one of the first in the country to spotlight vegetarian dishes, and this coincided with Benoît opening one of the first secular cooking schools in Quebec, Fumet de la vieille France, which she ran in the restaurant at night. She had to feed all those students somehow! After a fire in 1942, Benoît parted with the restaurant, going on to appear regularly on television and radio, publish more than 30 cookbooks and write the first encyclopedia of Canadian cuisine.

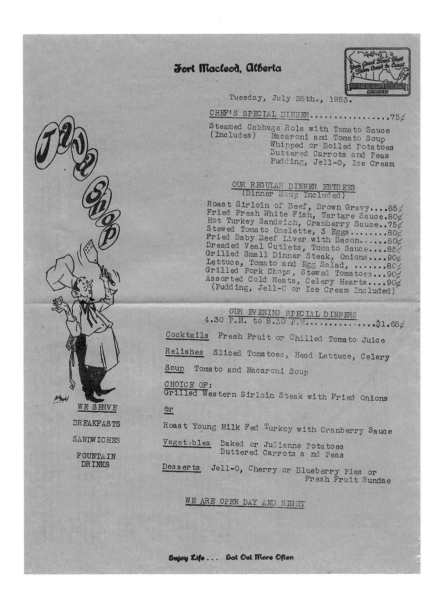

Fort Macleod, Alberta

Tuesday, July 28th., 1953.

CHEF'S SPECIAL DINNER.................75¢
Steamed Cabbage Rolls with Tomato Sauce
(Includes)   Macaroni and Tomato Soup
              Whipped or Boiled Potatoes
              Buttered Carrots and Peas
              Pudding, Jell-O, Ice Cream

OUR REGULAR DINNER ENTREES
(Dinner Soup Included)

Roast Sirloin of Beef, Brown Gravy....85¢
Fried Fresh White Fish, Tartare Sauce.80¢
Hot Turkey Sandwich, Cranberry Sauce..75¢
Stewed Tomato Omelette, 3 Eggs........80¢
Fried Baby Beef Liver with Bacon......80¢
Breaded Veal Cutlets, Tomato Sauce....85¢
Grilled Small Dinner Steak, Onions....90¢
Lettuce, Tomato and Egg Salad, ...80¢
Grilled Pork Chops, Stewed Tomatoes...90¢
Assorted Cold Meats, Celery Hearts....90¢
(Pudding, Jell-O or Ice Cream Included)

OUR EVENING SPECIAL DINNERS
4.30 P.M. to 8.30 P.M...............$1.65¢

Cocktails Fresh Fruit or Chilled Tomato Juice

Relishes Sliced Tomatoes, Head Lettuce, Celery

Soup Tomato and Macaroni Soup

CHOICE OF:
Grilled Western Sirloin Steak with Fried Onions

or

Roast Young Milk Fed Turkey with Cranberry Sauce

Vegetables Baked or Julienne Potatoes
            Buttered Carrots a nd Peas

Desserts Jell-O, Cherry or Blueberry Pies or
                       Fresh Fruit Sundae

WE ARE OPEN DAY AND NIGHT

Enjoy Life ... Eat Out More Often

WE SERVE
BREAKFASTS
SANDWICHES
FOUNTAIN
DRINKS

Wildcat Cafe

YELLOWKNIFE, NORTHWEST TERRITORIES (1937–2020)

It was gold and radium that brought the southerners to Yellowknife, the traditional lands of the Dene Nation. When Smokey Stout and Willie Wylie opened the Wildcat Cafe in 1937, the town was a mining camp with a few buildings. The log cabin that housed the Wildcat Cafe was a place for prospectors, furriers and bush pilots to stop in for a hot cup of coffee, down a big breakfast with slab bacon while sitting on the long wooden benches, and enjoy dinner plates filled with caribou and pickerel from Great Slave Lake. As one of the few restaurants in town, it quickly became a must-stop for visiting politicians, bankers and eventually travel writers and journalists writing about the mystique of the North.

When COVID-19 hit in 2020, the cafe was closed for the season, and in the 2021 season no one came forth to run it, so it continues to sit unoccupied save for some community events.

La Binerie Mont-Royal

MONTREAL, QUEBEC (1938–Present)

One dish that is baked into the Québécois psyche is beans. La Binerie could have been one among many places serving up fèves au lard, as Quebecers have done for generations, but their baked beans are so good, they have had a loyal following for almost a century. Joachim Lussier opened the restaurant in June 1938, intending to serve Québécois-style homey meals with a focus on beans—those little legume pearls spent 18 hours in the oven before hitting the heavy white plate. Since then, 23 seats have hosted hundreds of hungry patrons as they consumed beans, big breakfasts, tourtière, ragoût de boulettes and pâté chinois. In 2019, after decades of new owners, Jocelyne and Philippe Brunet took over and moved La Binerie from its original location onto rue Saint-Denis, quadrupling the seating but bringing the original stools and lunch counter along with them.

Wildcat Cafe circa 1938

Moishes

MONTREAL, QUEBEC (1938–2020)

You might have called it the Romanian steak row, in the 1930s. The Romanian Jews who had immigrated to Canada and settled in the Plateau neighbourhood along Saint-Laurent—known then as The Main—opened places like the Bucharest Grill and Moishes, serving up charcoal-grilled meats, alongside Schwartz's and its smoked meat. But Moishes outlasted them all.

Moishe Lighter immigrated to Canada in 1925, and it was his lucky poker hand that changed the dining scene in Montreal forever: he was working at Saffrin's restaurant in 1938 as a waiter when he won the restaurant from the gambling owner and fired up the grills under the new name of Romanian Paradise. But in 1940, when his home country sided with the Axis powers, he changed it to Moishes Charcoal Broiling House, stating he would revert to the old name when Romania was free and a paradise again, which didn't happen for a long time (in 1970, because of the Quebec language charter, it became Moishes).

Under the tin ceiling, diners enjoyed filet mignons for $1.50 and martinis for 60 cents as vested servers crisscrossed the dining room with trays of Monte Carlo potatoes and shrimp cocktail. By then, "Moishes" was a household word in Montreal and across the country for charcoal-grilled steaks and coleslaw so famous, you've been able to buy a huge tub of it at Costco since 2001.

The restaurant left the family in 2019 when Sportscene Group purchased it from Lighter's children and closed it in 2020, telling the press it was moving locations. At the time of writing, it has yet to reopen in its reconceived form in the Caisse de dépôt et placement du Québec building on Place Jean-Paul-Riopelle.

Rae and Jerry's

WINNIPEG, MANITOBA (1939–Present)

Most Winnipeggers know Rae and Jerry's as the gastronomical gem still serving up old-school steak dinners, with appetizers made tableside. It's a classic, cool and carnivorous experience. But most people don't know that the original owners, John Rae and Jerry Hemsworth, started their restaurant endeavour in 1939 in Brathwaite's Pharmacy, at 401 Portage Avenue. The classic steakhouse we know today opened in its then new location just down the street in 1957, after the pair spent more than $100,000 (that's equivalent to just under $1 million today) building the large restaurant and outfitting it with dark red plush booths, mirrored surfaces and an abstract mural of crabs, fish, plates and forks. The decor remains the same today, and many view the spot as an architectural gem as well as a gastronomical one. Current owner Steve Hrousalas took over in 1975 and has kept the institution status of Rae and Jerry's alive and well, maintaining the *Mad Men* vibe, and continuing to serve steaks and prime rib with a side of chilled tomato juice.

GOOD FOOD

Norman's
L.H. NORMAN, PROP.

MEATLESS TUESDAY   *Oct. 19/43*

PRICES INCLUDE CHOICE OF APPETIZER OR SOUP, VEGETABLES,
AND DESSERT
SERVED FROM 5 P.M. TO 8 P.M.
TOMATO SALAD 10¢ EXTRA

CONSOMME   OLD FASHIONED BEAN SOUP

FISH
FRIED OR BROILED

HADDOCK..40	MACKEREL 40
FISH CAKES 35	TUNA 40
FILLET OF SOLE.40	HALIBUT..50

KIPPERED HERRING, 40
BAKED HALIBUT 50
BOILED HADDOCK & EGG SAUCE..40
BAKED STUFFED HADDOCK 40

ENTREE
PLAIN OMELETTE
TOMATO OMELETTE .45
CHEESE OMELETTE 45
SPANISH OMELETTE 45
MACARONI & CHEESE.35
FRICCASSEE OF CHICKEN,55

SALADS
EGG & TOMATO SALAD 40
VEGETABLE SALAD 40

CHAPTER SIX

The 1940s

"Animals at the zoo
go meatless, too."

The cover page of *The Winnipeg Tribune* on May 4, 1943, featured a photograph of Nero the lion of the Winnipeg Zoo being fed a scoop of cold porridge by his keeper, George Grantham. Nero was quoted as saying "Ugh!" The corresponding article's title, "Animals At Zoo Go Meatless, Too," succinctly sums up the restaurant industry during the Second World War. The week before Nero made the front page, the Wartime Prices and Trade Board decreed that public eating places across the country would initiate Meatless Tuesday, meaning that, as part of the war effort, restaurants could not sell red meat to their patrons, something that lasted until 1947. This meant that beef, pork and lamb were off-limits, but not fish and fowl, so fish burgers became a popular menu item at cafes across the country. There were also prohibitions on the sale of iced cakes, hot dog buns and sliced bread, and inside a restaurant, diners were allowed only one-third of an ounce of butter each, and no more than one cup of coffee or tea.

But during the war there was a shift in the restaurant industry. A lot of the best cuts of meat and the best produce went to restaurants, so mostly it was the wealthy who ate well. With many staff off at war, the industry grappled with labour shortages, yet sales were at an all-time high, going from under $50 million before the war to $210 million. But for Japanese Canadians, life was not as fortuitous. Many of the shops and restaurants they owned were shut down and the population was forced into internment camps.

In the 1940s, car travel and paved highways became commonplace, and when people drive long distances, they gotta stop to eat. Enter the roadside diner. During this period, big neon signs with short words or phrases became popular out of necessity; with widening streets and speeding cars passing by, you needed to draw in customers with bold colours, shapes and lights. After the Second World War, waves of immigration shifted the dining landscape in Canada forever. Once the Chinese Exclusion Act was abolished in 1947, the Chinese restaurant scene exploded across the country, as did the number of Greek-owned pizza places and Italian delis. Meanwhile, tourism boards encouraged restaurateurs to redefine their dishes like butter tarts and back bacon as "Canadian," despite them being mostly regional.

The Chickenburger

HALIFAX, NOVA SCOTIA (1940–Present)

If you drove along the Bedford Highway on the way in or out of Halifax sometime between the 1940s and, well, yesterday, chances are you've stopped at The Chickenburger. What started as a roadside venue with a walk-up window and a neon rooster sign has become a Halifax institution. Jack and Bernice Innes flicked on the Open sign at The Chickenburger in 1940 on the spot Jack's father had run a food stand in the 1930s, after being inspired by those he had seen on a visit to Coney Island.

The couple started by selling hot dogs, hamburgers and chicken rolls for five cents, but by 1943 as wartime rationing started affecting restaurants' offerings, they were allowed to increase their menu by one item. They opted to put their steamed chicken on a hamburger bun and thus their iconic dish was born: the chickenburger, a simple homemade bun topped with cut-up steamed chicken. For more than 80 years now, The Chickenburger has been one of the most polarizing dishes for Haligonians, as there are those who love it (and have their own unique condiment combinations) and those who stick to the famous-in-their-own-right hamburgers and milkshakes.

Beautys Luncheonette

MONTREAL, QUEBEC (1942–Present)

When 21-year-old Hymie Sckolnick bought the Bancroft Snack Bar at the corner of Mont-Royal and Saint-Urbain in 1942, he probably didn't think he would end up in a court case surrounding a breakfast dish inspired by his wife, Freda. Together they had started pumping out breakfast and lunch to patrons living in the Plateau and nearby workers of the Jewish garment district. The restaurant's name was officially changed to Beautys—after Hymie's bowling nickname—in the 1970s because it had become such a landmark and everyone called it that.

The menu featured dishes like the Beautys Special, a breakfast sandwich made with a St-Viateur bagel, homemade cream cheese, smoked salmon, tomato and onion. The Mish-Mash, an omelette with sliced-up hot dog, salami, green peppers and fried onion, was trademarked by Sckolnick in 1989, but that trademark was enforced only in recent years when the couple sent out a round of cease-and-desist letters to other Montreal diners using the dish's name. Today, the business continues to be family-run—with their son Larry and his daughters, Elana and Julie, at the helm—and the Mish-Mash a breakfast fixture.

Chan's Restaurant

SUMMERSIDE, PRINCE EDWARD ISLAND (1941–1959)

The restaurants and shops of Summerside did very well during the Second World War, thanks to the influx of patrons from the Royal Canadian Air Force base and flight training school just outside the town. And the cover of the menu at Chan's "Restaurant of Distinction" from 1944 is very much a product of the time. The Summerside eatery menu featured four world leaders—Chiang Kai-shek, FDR, Churchill and Stalin—on its leather-bound cover.

Chan's was one of the first Chinese-owned cafes in the province to serve North Americanized Chinese dishes like chicken chop suey, chicken yet ca mein, pork foo young and chicken chow mein. No rice was to be found other than in the fried rice dish itself; all main dishes came with "Bread, Butter, French Fried Potatoes, Tea, coffee or milk." Later, in the 1950s, it would also serve Italian dishes, along with an array of seafood—mandatory on a Prince Edward Island menu no matter the decade—such as clam stew, fried haddock and lobster salad.

Bennett's Bakery

THUNDER BAY, ONTARIO (1940s–Present)

As the story goes, John Joseph "Black Jack" Pershing, a famous US general who fought in the First World War, came by Bennett's Bakery in the early 1940s and the owner, Art Bennett, decided to name a pastry after him. And so the Persian, a cinnamon bun–doughnut hybrid coated in bright pink icing, was born. Mario Nucci's family took over the bakery in 1964 and made the treat even more popular when, in 1992, they started a chain of coffee shops called The Persian Man, which now doles them out by the dozen at their bakery and deli, along with soups and sandwiches. The Persian Man sells three types of Persians: blueberry, chocolate and the one with classic pink-hued frosting. Is it cherry, is it strawberry, is it raspberry? The recipe is under lock and key at the bakery, so we will probably never know. But one thing is for sure: it satisfies the sweet tooth of Thunder Bay, as does their much-loved lemon slices and Sally Anns.

Restaurant of Distinction

Chan's Restaurant, Summerside, P.E.I.

Nanking Tavern and Restaurant

TORONTO, ONTARIO (1945–1980)

On any given Saturday night during hockey season, it wasn't abnormal to see Montreal Canadiens and Toronto Maple Leafs players sitting shoulder to shoulder amicably, scarfing down chop suey at Nanking Restaurant, at 75–77 Elizabeth Street. The Leafs' Tim Horton and the "Big M," Frank Mahovlich and Bernie "Boom Boom" Geoffrion from the Habs would dine on steaks and Cantonese-style dishes after patrons watched them play on the black-and-white TVs above the bar that were always tuned into the game.

Opened by the Lee family in 1945, Nanking was one of the first of the "Big Four" restaurants that established Chinatown eateries as part of Toronto's dining scene for non-Chinese people. Nanking was followed by the famed Lichee Gardens, opened by Harry Lem in 1948, which could seat three hundred

people and became an institution, and the two golden-age restaurants, Sai Woo in 1953, and Jean Lumb's Kwong Chow which opened in 1959. All four became popular once the Chinese community was recognized properly after the annulment of the Chinese Exclusion Act in 1947.

Nanking was the first restaurant in Chinatown to get a liquor licence from the LLBO, meaning it didn't need to resort to selling "cold tea"—otherwise known as beer or whisky—from teapots, like the rest of the neighbourhood's restaurants. By early 1950, the bar menu at Nanking was almost as large as the dinner menu, serving cocktails like the Morning Glory Fizz (50 cents) and the Gimlet (60 cents). Dinner for two with chicken noodle soup, egg rolls, chicken chop suey with mushrooms, pork fried rice and Chinese pastries would set your date back $1.70.

Toad River Lodge

TOAD RIVER, BRITISH COLUMBIA (1947–Present)

After the Alaskan-Canadian Highway was completed in 1942, the lodgings left by US army crews who built it were turned into public lodges offering up fuel, hot meals and a place to sleep. Within three years of the highway opening to public traffic, more than fifty thousand tourists drove it each year and, in its heyday, the 1,800-mile strip was known as the longest Main Street in North America. Those lodges became so much more than mileposts; the lodge was a lifeline for the local population, and the spot for Saturday night dances, debates over hot coffee, and the community centre.

The Callison brothers, Lash and Dennis, along with their wives Winnie and Marj respectively, opened Toad River Lodge in 1947, in Toad River at mile 422. When it first was listed in the inaugural issue of *The Milepost* (the essential lodge guide still published today), Toad River Lodge didn't even have hot water, but it did offer guided hunting. Throughout the decades, the generator-run lodge expanded to include a 14-unit motel, a cafe, a service station and now an RV park and gift shop.

The cafe serves up typical lodge meals: hearty, home-cooked eats like beef chili, elk burgers, pork chops and huge pieces of pie with three scoops of ice cream, all prepared using the electricity that was finally installed in 2012 by BC Hydro.

Vie's Chicken and Steak House

VANCOUVER, BRITISH COLUMBIA (1948–1979)

A small old house with a big neon sign that shone brightly all night long brought revellers and steak eaters to Vie's Chicken and Steak in Vancouver's Strathcona neighbourhood. The rickety house, with its red and yellow ceilings, probably smelled of fried chicken fat most nights. Vie and her husband Bob Moore opened their restaurant at 209 Union Street in 1948, at the corner of Hogan's Alley, and it soon became a cornerstone of the city's Black community. Open every night until really late—from 5 p.m. to 5 a.m.—it had no liquor licence; Vie provided the ice and the mix when things got going, usually after midnight. Vie hired only women; Jimi Hendrix's grandmother was the cook for two decades, serving up pan-fried steaks, half chickens, homemade biscuits, along with fries, mushrooms, onions and black-eyed peas, to the likes of Ella Fitzgerald, Duke Ellington and Lena Horne when they passed through town, not to mention the local cops and cabbies getting off shift. Always welcoming, always good hot food. Vie died in 1975, leaving her daughter to run the place until it closed on September 25, 1979.

Pizzeria Napoletana

MONTREAL, QUEBEC (1948–Present)

With an influx of second-wave Italians to Montreal's Little Italy neighbourhood after the Second World War, this Jean Talon Market–adjacent area became a happening place. When Pizzeria Napoletana opened its doors on the corner of Dante and avenue de Gaspé in 1948, it had only five tables where diners could eat one—or both—of the two types of pizza on the menu. Most patrons hung out to play pool or to have a cup of coffee with a familiar face. The restaurant was purchased by the Girolamo family in 1980 and, now with more than 20 types of pizzas on the menu, remains a staple Italian eatery in Montreal.

Pizzeria Napoletana, 1970s

ROUND UP
CAFE
LAW OFFICE
LAW OFFICE
D. F. KENNEDY
BARRISTER SOLICITOR
NOTARY
WO-1-3531
Debby Anne
SHOPPE
Whalley Cyclery
BICYCLES
and RADIO REPAIRS
AUTO
PARTS
7up
CANADA'S
BRITISH PIPE TOBACCO
LAW OFF.
WO 1-7787

Round Up Cafe

SURREY, BRITISH COLUMBIA (1949–2021)

A chance glance at a newspaper ad brought Goldie Springenatic and her husband, Orest, to the Whalley neighbourhood of Surrey to purchase the Round Up Cafe in 1959, and it was the community they built that made them stay. They bought the place from Len Goodmanson, who built it along the King George Boulevard, a major thoroughfare in the 1940s and '50s; the diner's neon sign was meant to attract hungry motorists.

Along with being foundational to the local baseball community, the Springenatic's 24-hour diner became a landmark restaurant in Whalley, serving up big plates of perogies and cabbage rolls, along with diner classics like Monte Cristo sandwiches, lemon meringue pie and hearty breakfasts. By the 1980s, they were offering a Ukrainian smorgasbord for $8 a person on Fridays and Saturdays. The restaurant closed in 2021, stating that the COVID-19 pandemic broke them.

Left: Round Up Cafe, 1950s

Please Do Not Deface This Menu

CHAPTER SEVEN

The 1950s

"The combination of a postwar economic boom and an influx of immigration was the perfect climate for many new restaurants to flourish across Canada."

In December 1955, the *Toronto Star* covered the grand opening of the first Japanese restaurant in Canada, the House of Fuji-Matsu, at 17 Elm Street, off Yonge. The article describes the 12 kimono-clad hostesses teaching shoeless diners sitting at low cedar tables on tatami mats how to use chopsticks, and staying by their side throughout the whole meal. Patrons embarked on a "new dining adventure," as the manager Tony Shiozaki described his intentions to show Canadians the culture of Japan and "cement good relations between that country and Canadians."

The House of Fuji-Matsu survived only three years, but it was the first of many firsts. The combination of a postwar economic boom and an influx of Italian, Hungarian, Chinese, Japanese and Eastern European immigration was the perfect climate for many new restaurants and all kinds of new-to-them dishes to flourish across Canada. Heading into the 1950s, restaurant dining was, for most Canadians, still an act of necessity: breakfast at a tearoom,

hotel or diner meant they were travelling, a hot lunch somewhere downtown meant it was during work hours or they were at a department store doing some shopping.

But dining for novelty was growing increasingly popular with the rise of drive-ins and middle-class family restaurants, and as more cuisines became available—though the hot turkey sandwich, the hamburger and french fries were still menu dominators as malt shops sprung up seemingly everywhere. Takeout menus, take-home meals and drive-ins became important factors when middle-class families decided what they were going to eat for dinner. Meanwhile, technological advancements during the Second World War like freeze-dried foods, paper food containers and even plastic wrap facilitated the rise of the chain restaurant and standardization among franchises, paving the way for several of the national chains we know today—they're why those fries taste the same at every location across the country, and why they're in the same iconic paper cup.

Ches's Famous Fish and Chips

ST. JOHN'S, NEWFOUNDLAND AND LABRADOR

(1951–Present)

If a small town in Newfoundland and Labrador has a restaurant at all, chances are it will be either a Chinese-Canadian restaurant or a snack bar serving fish and chips (or sometimes both, if the town is big enough), both sporting the iconic backlit Pepsi-sponsor sign. There are few smells better than the one you experience when you peel away the brown paper wrapping and dig into a two-piece Fi and Chi with D and G and a can of DP, local shorthand for fish and chips with dressing and gravy on the fries and a Diet Pepsi. And while fish and chips are today an ingrained part of Newfoundland and Labrador's culinary tradition, they didn't enter the canon until after the First World War. Soldiers returning from Europe had tried fish and chips on leave in London, England, and legend has it that a man named Stacey was the first to sell fish and chips from his coal-fuelled, horse-drawn food cart, which he had imported from Germany.

Ches and Betty Barbour were among the first to open a brick-and-mortar shop—on Harvey Road in St. John's in October 1951—and legitimize the British street food as a restaurant meal. Every morning from April to January, Ches would get into his boat, sail out the narrows to catch the fish, then upon his return fillet, fry and sell it with chips for 30 cents (he was also the first in the city to debone the fish for sale). Eventually, the couple moved up the road to Freshwater, where their location still stands today.

Over the years the business expanded, with a location on Gower Street in 1968 (it was torn down in 1974 because the newly constructed Trans-Canada Highway barrelled right through) then to Topsail Road, Mount Pearl, and then eventually past the overpass to more than 10 locations across the province.

In 1992, the cod moratorium devastated the province and many of its fish-and-chips shops; Ches's shifted gears and increased prices for the fresh fish they had to now get from the south coast. To this day, their restaurants still post a sign in the window saying whether the fish is fresh or frozen.

Top: Ches Barbour in the first location on Harvey Road

Braeburn Lodge

BRAEBURN, YUKON (1952–Present)

The Overland Trail between Dawson City and Whitehorse was full of road-houses at the turn of the century, and they all were always expected to serve up a good meal. By the 1950s, construction of the Klondike Highway was underway, and while many of those early roadhouses disappeared once the highway replaced the trail, a few remain, including the Braeburn Lodge, famous for its sour-dough cinnamon buns, made by current owner Steve Watson and his small staff. Those buns are so famous, in fact, that Whitehorse pilots looking for a little (or big) snack on a pleasure flight will land on the small airstrip in Braeburn, affectionately named the Cinnamon Bun Airstrip. As the penultimate stop of the Yukon Quest sled dog race, Braeburn Lodge bakes up dozens of orders to fuel racers every February.

Roma Bakery & Deli

HAMILTON, ONTARIO (1952–Present)

This Italian deli's pizza is very much an "if you know, you know" thing. "Cult-like" is a strong term, but those giant boxes containing their huge slabs of cheese-less pizza (21 inches long, in fact) are found at every gathering in the Hamilton area, and it seems to be something that no one knows about until you live there.

It was a trip to Rome in early 1950 that spurred Philip DiFilippo to develop Hamilton's favourite party food. DiFilippo, whose parents emigrated from Abruzzo, Italy, in 1910, left Stelco, Hamilton's steelworks, in 1952 to open the bakery with his wife, Pauline, whose parents emigrated from Sicily in 1912. Initially, they sold only bread to the city's Italian community, because most Italians made their own pizza. Until the 1970s, the pizza wasn't very popular at all, and the DiFilippo children were raised to hide their Italian heritage in fear of local discrimination—they didn't even speak Italian, and like many families hid their winemaking, meat curing and tomato canning.

Roma delivery van from the 1950s

The family thanks Pierre Trudeau's official statement on multiculturalism as a turning point for them; they moved to the flagship location in 1976, and that is when the pizza cult really took off. Then and now, the pizza is light and fluffy, but not mushy, with a perfectly spiced, savoury San Marzano tomato sauce. The recipe may seem simple, but there is no replicating it: it's a secret recipe, with no cheese, sugar or meat, and meant to be served at room temperature. And Hamiltonians love it; these days, the third generation of DiFilippos, with Phil Jr. at the helm, sells about three thousand pizzas a week at the flagship store and at more than 20 local grocery stores.

The Steak Loft

EDMONTON, ALBERTA (1952–1981)

Was Mitch Klimove's steak the one that inspired the Hy's carnivorous dynasty? Rumour has it that after his friend Hy Aisenstat visited the Steak Loft in the early 1950s, he decided to open his own steakhouse in Calgary above a women's clothing store, and the rest is meaty history. Klimove, the son of Russian Jewish immigrants, opened The Steak Loft on Jasper Avenue in late 1952. One of the first ads to appear in the *Edmonton Journal* promised that if you could eat the 72-ounce top sirloin steak (regular price $9.50) in one sitting, you could get it for free.

With live music from a quartet flown in from New York reverberating off the dark wood and velvet decor, oblong platters filled with dry-aged filet mignon (8 ounces for $2) were paired with table-side Caesar salad, shrimp cocktail and Maryland fried chicken, not to mention chicken cacciatore and rigatoni with meatballs—this place was always bopping, and so was Klimove's Old Bailey Lounge downstairs.

The restaurant burnt down in 1981, and two years later Aisenstat and Klimove teamed up to open Hy's Steak Loft, a favourite in the city for almost three decades now.

The Paddlewheel

WINNIPEG, MANITOBA (1954–2013)

The wheels of the faux paddle fountain started turning in October 1954. The new cafeteria-style restaurant becoming all the rage in 1950s Winnipeg was initially called the Paddle Wheel Buffet and was decorated in a riverboat and prairie theme highlighting "the Red River's most romantic era, the colourful days of the old paddle steamer," according to the ads. Think prairie-landscape murals adorning the walls and clapboard siding of faux homesteads in the corners and dividing dining room spaces.

Patrons in the main dining room would grab a now-iconic veneer lunch tray sporting a "The Bay" logo, sliding it along the stainless-steel rails as they made their way past the displays of roast turkey dinners, hamburgers and shelves lined with dessert glasses filled with ice cream or Jell-O and whipped cream. They'd then enjoy their meal on the sixth floor of the Hudson's Bay Company on Portage Avenue. In addition to the main dining area, workers took advantage of the snack counter to bring hot coffee and sandwiches back to the office. In the 1950s, deals were made over roast beef in the Men's Saloon, and in the Crinoline Court, ladies shared luncheon gossip. Generations of families ventured downtown to shop and dined at the Paddlewheel, and the decor hadn't changed much by the time it closed in 2013.

The Paddlewheel restaurant, located on the 6th floor of the HBC Winnipeg downtown store

Foo's Ho Ho

VANCOUVER, BRITISH COLUMBIA (1954–2015)

On a Saturday night in Vancouver's Chinatown in the 1950s, you would be bedazzled by all the neon. After the movies or seeing a live show, throngs of people would flock to East Pender Street for a meal of Cantonese specialities at places like Ming's, Bamboo Terrace and Marco Polo—and Ho Ho Chop Suey House, which had its grand opening on February 18, 1954, on the first two floors of the Sun Ah Hotel building at 102 East Pender.

It was operated by the Quon family, who claimed their food was "prepared under rigid sanitary conditions by expert Cantonese Chefs in the most modern stainless-steel kitchen on the Pacific Coast." The neon sign was special: a bowl of steaming chop suey gave way to the words "Ho Ho" flickering back and forth between English and Chinese characters. Like other Chinatown eateries, they stayed open until at least 3 a.m., steaming bowls of sweet-and-sour soup, omelette-sized egg foo young and duck salad making its way around the dining room.

In the late 1990s, an influx of people from Hong Kong shifted Chinatown, and the allure of the fading neon signs diminished. The restaurant was taken over by Joanne and James Sam, who changed the name to Foo's Ho Ho in 1998 in honour of James's father, Kwok Sam, who cooked at and managed several Chinatown institutions, like Foo's.

Left: Foo's Ho Ho circa 1973

Swiss Chalet

CANADA-WIDE (1954–Present)

What does rotisserie chicken have to do with Switzerland? In Canada, more than you might think. In 1954, 20-year-old Richard Mauran came to Toronto with the vision of opening a version of the rotisserie chicken restaurant where he'd learned the business from father Maurice Mauran's Chalet BBQ in Montreal, an institution in its own right. He borrowed $25,000 from his father and opened the Swiss Chalet Bar-B-Q at 234 Bloor Street West, in Toronto, near the Varsity Theatre, with its alpine decor (inspired by his Swiss-born father's heritage)—dark wood panelling, wooden beams and fake interior windows with frilly curtains. A quarter chicken was 25 cents.

From the beginning, the roasted chicken dinners were served with a dipping sauce, which these days is lovingly (or distastefully) referred to as Chalet Sauce. Not quite a gravy, not quite a condiment, it's a salty-savoury sauce with hues of Thanksgiving and Christmas. Love it or hate it, the Chalet Sauce is a part of our history. Oh, and did I mention Rick also founded Harvey's, five years later?

The Candlelite

ST. JOHN'S, NEWFOUNDLAND AND LABRADOR
(1955–1976)

Many a first date was had at The Candlelite on Harvey Road. In the 1950s, there weren't a lot of "nice places" in St. John's to take a date on a Friday night or for a special occasion meal, but this spot, with its mini jukeboxes in the booths and individual-sized silver teapots, was a great option either before or after a movie at the Paramount, just down the street. It was frequented by university students, so much so that the gossip column in the 1961 *Muse* (the Memorial University student newspaper) mentioned an engineering student named Wayne who cheaped out with his date and didn't order her any dessert—she ate cookies from her purse!

Seal flipper pie dinners, fresh lobster, and rabbit pie were regular specials advertised in the daily paper, but people fondly remember the steaks, coconut cream pie, milkshakes and 55-cent hamburgers. And word on the street was you could bring your bowl to the kitchen door at the back and they would fill it with french fries for 50 cents.

Junior's

WINNIPEG, MANITOBA (1956–Present)

A question that's sure to get the juices flowing in Winnipeg is this: Who has the best Fat Boy in town? Whether you love Junior's, VJ's, Dairi Wip or RedTop, one thing is certain: the burger—a sloppy mess of a hamburger patty topped with secret-recipe chili, quartered dill pickle,

onions, mustard and a lot of mayonnaise—was made by a Greek Canadian.

Gus and George Scouras immigrated to Canada in the early 1950s while they were in their teens, amid civil war in their home country of Greece. After working at their uncle's restaurant in Thunder Bay, it was Gus who opened Junior's in 1956, where he put that chili-topped burger on the menu as the Lotta Burger. George followed suit by opening Big Boy restaurant with the burger by the same name. While the Scouras brothers are more than likely the inventors of the burger itself, it's Mike Lambos, who bought the Dairi Wip Drive In in 1959 after a stint working at Big Boy, who came up with the name. Whichever you choose, it'll be messy and delicious, and you'll probably need to eat it with a knife and fork.

Marie-Antoinette Restaurant & Tahiti Bar

SAINTE-ANNE-DE-BEAUPRÉ, QUEBEC (1956–1982)

The chain of 24-hour diners in Quebec called Marie-Antoinette were not named after the famous doomed monarch but the founder who started it all in 1956, Marie-Antoinette Letellier. At their peak, there were more than a dozen locations in Quebec, three of which had tiki bars. The one opened by her son, Jean Letellier, in Sainte-Anne-de-Beaupré outlasted them all and is now Le Marie Beaupré Restaurant. The menu items at Marie-Antoinette were on par with those of other diners that opened during that time: club sandwiches, chicken and the famous Tom Pouce burger, with its special house-made sauce (named after the famous General Tom Thumb). But in the Tahiti Bar, Letellier latched onto the popularity of tiki bars with drinks like the Brise D'Hawaii, Scorpion, Aloha Daiquiri and the Nuit Tropicale, served to imbibers in beautiful ceramic tiki glasses (now collectors' items) by women adorned with leis.

Rum Breeze

Recipe inspired by Tahiti Bar at Marie-Antoinette

The tiki cocktail craze began in the 1930s but really took off in the 1950s and 1960s, resulting in Polynesian-themed restaurants and bars with bamboo decor and coloured lanterns popping up across North America. The Mai Tai, Piña Colada and Bahama Mama entered the cocktail canon, which can still be found on many bar menus today. In recent years, tiki cocktail bars have had a revival, with the Shameful Tiki Room in Toronto and Le Mal Nécessaire in Montreal. This cocktail is an iteration of Trader Vic's Punch meets Rum Runner, meant for a hot day.

1. Add all the ingredients to a shaker with ice and shake until well chilled. The shaker should be cold to the touch.

2. Strain into a stubby glass filled with crushed ice.

3. Garnish with a skewered brandied cherry or a pineapple wedge.

DEMERARA SIMPLE SYRUP

1. Put the demerara sugar and water in a small saucepan set over medium heat. Bring the mixture to a simmer, stirring often, until the sugar is dissolved, 2 to 3 minutes, and the mixture has thickened ever so slightly.

2. Remove the syrup from the heat and let cool completely.

3. Store in a sealed glass jar in the fridge for up to 1 month.

SERVES 1

- 1½ ounces (45 ml) blackstrap rum
- 1½ ounces (45 ml) light rum
- 3 Tbsp (45 ml) pineapple juice
- 2 Tbsp (30 ml) lime juice, freshly squeezed
- 1 Tbsp (15 ml) orange juice, freshly squeezed
- 1 Tbsp (15 ml) demerara syrup (see below)
- 1 tsp (5 ml) orgeat syrup or grenadine
- Brandied cherry or pineapple wedge, for garnish

MAKES 1½ CUPS (375 ML) SYRUP

- 1 cup (250 ml) demerara or turbinado sugar
- 1 cup (250 ml) water

Ardmore Tea Room

HALIFAX, NOVA SCOTIA (1958–Present)

The Ardmore Tea Room has been a staple on Quinpool Road for more than 50 years, but the Cormier family started their Ardmore empire on Liverpool Street. Tennyson and Norma Cormier opened the Ardmore Grill in 1952 and expanded quickly, opening another location on Gottingen Street in 1955. A year after buying an old drugstore on the corner of Elm and Quinpool, where they launched the Ardmore Tea Room, they decided to put all their efforts into the one location, which has since become an institution.

From the day the tearoom opened, the stools at the low counter and booths were filled with high-school kids sipping on cherry Cokes and families downing chips doused with gravy. Eggs Benedict, western omelettes, hot turkey sandwiches and burger platters served on heavy white plates top Formica tabletops at the Ardmore, which is still in the family— Mike Cormier runs things now.

New Glasgow Lobster Suppers

NEW GLASGOW, PRINCE EDWARD ISLAND (1958–Present)

The radio announcer on Ocean 100 has been re-recording the same ad for "mile-high lemon meringue pie" at the New Glasgow Lobster Suppers for decades. What started as a Junior Farmers fundraiser is now a must-have culinary experience on the Island. Twelve of those Junior Farmers took over operations in 1972, taking the supper from a fundraiser to a restaurant business. By 1980, it was run by just four of them: the two couples who started it all, William and Thelma Nicholson, and Jean and Sterling MacRae.

The place has been open since 1958, and it hasn't changed much since (they got a POS system only five years ago, after much debate). The same woman has been baking those lemon meringue pies, along with a mountain of rolls, for at least 30 years. Here you'll find the organized chaos of a community, with teenagers in T-shirts heaving away plastic buckets of empty mussel shells from long communal tables lined with checkered tablecloths, at each seat a paper placemat printed with instructions on how to eat lobster (the only difference between now and then is that these cartoony cards have their own Instagram account). The endless bowls of chowder in Styrofoam, the plastic bibs, the giant lobsters, the bottomless soda. It's all like it always was.

The first New Glasgow Lobster Suppers building, 1958

Hungarian Village

TORONTO, ONTARIO (1959–1987)

Toronto's Annex neighbourhood is filled with students, dive bars and Thai restaurants, but its strip of Bloor Street West was once known as the Goulash Archipelago. When Hungary fell to a Communist regime in 1956, Toronto saw an influx of Hungarians who were ready to start cooking (more than twelve thousand of the almost forty thousand Hungarians who immigrated to Canada ended up in Toronto). Blue Cellar Room, Emke Hungarian and Little Korona lined Bloor, while Hungarian Village opened, in 1959, on Bay Street just east of the Annex.

From beginning, Levente and Erika Vámossy and Irene Kölcze's dishes at Hungarian Village—Attila's Flaming Platter piled high with roasted meats on a spit, salads arranged in lettuce cups, and the Transylvania wood platter with schnitzel and sausages—were adored by patrons, who devoured them while listening to traditional music played by violinists roaming around the restaurant, which was decorated with wooden beams and a bulbous white hearth. These days, the only restaurant remaining of this endangered species is Country Style on Bloor, which is still serving up nokedli with paprikash and plate-sized wiener schnitzel.

"Welcome to the Goulash Archipelago."

CHAPTER EIGHT

The 1960s

"Walter Chell was looking for inspiration and he found it at the bottom of his bowl of spaghetti alle vongole."

alter Chell was looking for inspiration and, in 1969, he found it at the bottom of his bowl of spaghetti alle vongole. As a bartender at the Calgary Inn, he had been asked to create a cocktail in celebration of the hotel's new Italian restaurant, Marco's. After three months of mixology experimentation, Chell created the Bloody Caesar, one of Canada's most recognizable and adored libations. Inspired by the pairing of clams and tomatoes in the Italian pasta dish spaghetti alle vongole, Chell decided to convert the combo into a cocktail by combining clam and tomato juices with vodka, adding a dash of Worcestershire sauce and rimming the glass with celery salt. Named after the Roman emperor (unlike the Tijuana-born salad), the Bloody Caesar is a homage to Chell's Italian heritage.

The Caesar might be considered Calgary's cocktail, but it is ironically Canadian—we drink more than 400 million of those savoury sippers every year!

By the middle of the 1960s, Canada finally had a national flag, and with more than one-third of the population with neither British nor French ancestors, multiculturalism was starting to take hold as a national concept, as well as at the dinner table. Dining out became trendier, and it grew important to be seen at the restaurant hotspots. In a 1959 *Maclean's* article predicting food trends for the 1960s, Ken Lefolii speculated that "new exotic foods will make more global gourmets." He was right about that, but he was wrong in his other prediction that Chinese food would go by the wayside in favour of Polynesian, as during the 1960s, Chinese restaurants multiplied tenfold. As did chain restaurants and doughnut shops. Dining in department stores evolved into restaurants inside a new thing called shopping malls. And as for the trend of Canadian champagne Lefolii envisioned? Not so much.

Joe's Lunch

SASKATOON, SASKATCHEWAN (1960–2006)

The old-school diner on 20th Street may have been famous for its sky-high deluxe burger, "a hand-squashed patty loaded with everything from mushrooms to cucumbers," but the magic of this place was all thanks to the Leung family who owned it. Choe "Joe" Leung immigrated to Canada from Guangzhou, China, in 1921 and spent decades working and operating restaurants in Saskatchewan

while separated from his wife, Yue Yek Leung, and their three children because of Canada's Chinese Exclusion Act. His two daughters died in China in the 1950s, but his son, David, finally came to Canada in 1952 and helped him work at his Paris Cafe. When Joe's wife came in 1959, they opened a restaurant on 20th Street and lived in the apartment upstairs.

Joe's Lunch opened its doors in 1960, serving up a simple menu of diner staples like cheeseburgers, milkshakes and Cantonese dishes. David married Gina, who emigrated from Hong Kong in the 1960s after a long-distance courtship set up by a cousin. It was her wonton soup that became as famous as their burger for the next four decades, until the place closed in 2006 when no one in the family wanted to carry on the business.

Golden Palace

OTTAWA, ONTARIO (1960–Present)

The open-ended question is: What is an Ottawa burnt-end egg roll? The bigger-than-average cannoli-esque egg roll is famous in the city, but at the grand opening of the Golden Palace on April 14, 1960, it was all about promoting the fancy, modern bungalow with piped-in music, air conditioning and turquoise walls. Tables were covered with white linens and intricately folded napkins, and diners enjoyed Chinese gow par (advertised as Hong Kong–style beefsteak), chow gim loo, and "bar-b-q" duck. The burnt-end egg rolls were on Golden Palace's very first menu, ringing in at 20 cents each, but it was years before those tasty cylinders became a phenomenon in the city. The open ends caused the filling of cabbage, celery, onions, bean sprouts and pork (plus a few secret ingredients that the Golden Palace won't reveal) to burn at the ends. The egg rolls are so synonymous with Ottawa that in 2013 when the Habs were playing the Sens in the first round of the Stanley Cup playoffs, Ottawa mayor Jim Watson made an egg roll/smoked meat bet to Montreal mayor Michael Applebaum on who would win the series. Does it get any more Canadian than two mayors having an Instagram fight over hockey and exchanging egg rolls and Montreal smoked meat?

Satellite Restaurant

CHATHAM-KENT, ONTARIO (1962–Present)

A chance stopover in Italy changed the pizza lovers' landscape of Canada forever. In 1954, the chain migration of Greeks to Canada was in full swing, and 20-year-old Sotirios "Sam" Panopoulos was on his way to Canada from his home in Vourvoura, Greece, when the boat docked in Naples, and he tasted the savoury pizza pie for the first time. It was love at first bite. When he opened the Satellite Restaurant in 1962 with his brother Nikitas (Nick), he knew pizza was going on the menu in addition to diner staples, even though it was still a relatively new food for Canadians. With the tiki craze also in full swing and some Chinese dishes already on the menu at the diner, Panopoulos one day tossed some canned pineapple he had sitting on the shelf, along with some cubed ham, overtop the dough and called it "Hawaiian pizza." The rest is history.

Aki Restaurant

VANCOUVER, BRITISH COLUMBIA (1963–2018)

Today, Vancouver has over six hundred sushi restaurants, but in the 1960s, Aki, the little shop at 374 Powell Street, was a ground-breaker and a rule-breaker. Aki Takeuchi was born in 1935 in nearby Steveston, a predominantly immigrant-populated fishing village filled with canneries, fisher people and Japanese families. When the town lost half its population due to the internment of Japanese Canadians in camps in 1942, Takeuchi and his family waited out the war in Osaka. Many Japanese Canadians returned to their homes in the early 1950s, but Aki settled in Vancouver. A trip to San Francisco made him realize he could make a sushi restaurant work in Vancouver, and after a five-year apprenticeship at a Japanese restaurant there, he set up shop.

Aki opened in 1963 on Powell Street (in what was then known as Japantown) with a four-person sushi bar and small screened rooms with tatami mats, serving sake out of teapots because they had no liquor licence. Initially, health inspectors were not down with the idea of raw fish being served, demanding that the sushi rice be served hot, but eventually he won them over. The restaurant moved to 745 Thurlow and was very popular throughout the 1970s and '80s, attracting movie stars and politicians alike, who lined up around the block to get in. Aki and his wife worked every single day the restaurant was open, until he died in 2013 after a battle with cancer.

In 2014, their son, Brian Takeuchi, took over and moved the restaurant to 1368 West Pender Street, where it became known for the robata grill, sukiyaki and tempura dishes that had been on the menu since Aki had first tried to convince health officials to chill out and eat raw fish.

Bill Wong's

MONTREAL, QUEBEC (1963–2007)

Bill Wong changed the way Montrealers ate Chinese food. Wong, born in Montreal to Chinese immigrant parents, was sent to China during the Depression. He returned at age 17, in 1937 and trained as an engineer at McGill University but decided he wanted to make lots of money instead and opened his first restaurant, House of Wong, on chemin Queen-Mary in 1955. It was a gamble because it wasn't in Chinatown and would have to rely completely on non-Chinese patrons—a first in the city for a Chinese restaurant. Thanks to Wong's ingenuity, including offering takeout and free delivery (a 1970 ad offered a free six-pack of Pepsi with telephone orders), House of Wong found success and he opened several more locations.

In 1963, he was offered a massive space on boulevard Décarie that he couldn't pass up. He opened Bill Wong's, which at first didn't do so well—Wong had to strategically place Chinese screens to make the enormous restaurant feel intimate. After a visit to a roast-beef buffet in Toronto for a family member's wedding rehearsal dinner, he realized how well the family-style dishes of Chinese cuisine would work as a buffet and convinced his investors to give that a try. By 1968, Bill Wong's was the place to dine on Décarie, with seven dining rooms, seating for a thousand and a $1.95 all-you-can-eat Chinese food buffet, the first in Montreal and probably Canada. It also served French and Canadian dishes, and fancy cocktails. The restaurant stayed open for 40 years, closing in 2007.

REPAS ET CONSOMMATIONS

Le Dragon
La salle à manger Le Dragon doit sa renommée à son buffet de 23 plats chauds et froids; vous apprécierez notre authentique cuisine de Canton et nos mets internationaux. Les groupes de 12 ou moins y trouveront facilement place.

Benihana
Un succulent repas japonais est préparé à votre table dans le plus pur style de l'hibachi traditionnel. C'est l'endroit idéal pour marier affaires et plaisir.

Le bar Son Vida
Plusieurs ententes ont été conclues dans l'atmosphère intime du Son Vida. Une agréable musique d'ambiance vous détendra et nos musiciens vous feront danser le soir.

SALLES PRIVÉES

Le Havre
Le gai salon au décor d'inspiration polynésienne peut recevoir des groupes de 30 personnes ou moins.

Salle Singapore
125 convives peuvent se régaler dans cette confortable salle de style marin au tapis luxueux.

Top O' Wong
Spacieuse et gaie, cette salle peut recevoir jusqu'à 225 invités. Vous utiliserez la scène pour exposer vos marchandises, installer la table d'honneur ou l'orchestre. Il y a une piste de danse et nous fournissons le piano.

Refuge du Son Vida
Coin idéal pour les réceptions et les réunions de petits groupes de 15 personnes et moins.

- Les salles peuvent s'agrandir pour recevoir 400 invités
- bar privé sur demande
- édifice climatisé
- vaste stationnement gratuit
- équipement audio-visuel des plus modernes à votre disposition sans frais

Appelez le directeur des réceptions à
731-8202

BILL WONG'S

7965, Décarie, angle Ferrier

7965 Decarie at Ferrier

DINING AND BAR FACILITIES

Le Dragon
Famous for its 23-dish hot and cold buffet; the finest classic Cantonese dishes; a lavish international menu. Booth parties for 12 or less.

Benihana Japanese Steak House
Succulent Japanese delicacies prepared at your table. Hibachi style. A great place to combine business with pleasure.

Son Vida Bar
Many a business deal is quietly settled in the intimate atmosphere of this sophisticated meeting place. Live music for listening or dancing.

PRIVATE ROOMS

Le Havre
Accommodates gatherings of 30 or less. A festive salon designed along Polynesian lines.

Singapore Room
A comfortable room that harbours 125 or less. Attractively decorated on a nautical theme. Luxuriously carpeted.

Top O' Wong
Spacious, bright and adaptable—accommodates groups up to 225. Built in stage for display use, dance band, head table. Dance floor; piano supplied.

Son Vida Hideaway
Ideal for small receptions, meetings—groups up to 15.

- Rooms may be opened up to accommodate up to 400.
- private bar facilities
- air conditioned throughout
- spacious free parking
- latest audio-visual equipment available without charge

Phone:
Banquet Manager,
731-8202.

The story of
The House of Wong Inc.

One of Montreal's largest and finest Chinese restaurants

Two years ago, "The House of Wong" opened as a small Chinese Restaurant at 5255 Queen Mary Road. Just three months after the opening, we greatly enlarged our premises to meet the public's demand for really high quality Chinese Food. For this happy state of affairs we owe our thanks to:

OUR CUSTOMERS
. . . for their appreciation and continued support.

OUR STAFF
. . . for their skilled and most capable service.

OUR SUPPLIERS
. . . for their dependability and constant co-operation. Listed below are some of our suppliers.

MEATS—
    CANADA PACKERS LTD.
GROCERIES—
    ABOOSAMBA KOURI INC.
VEGETABLES—
    CARIELICK WHOLESALE FRUIT REG'D.
DAIRY PRODUCTS—
    ERNEST COUSINS LTD.
FISH—
    WALDMAN'S FISH CO. LTD.
POULTRY—
    IDEAL POULTRY & EGG CO. LTD.
CHOP SUEYS—
    FOO LUNG CO.

PAPER & SANITARY SUPPLIES—
    HYGIENE PRODUCTS LTD. (MR. GANIME)
NOODLES—
    WING HING LUNG CO.
MATCHES—
    BOOK MATCH LTD.
CROCKERY—
    EMPIRE CROCKERY CO.
STORE FIXTURES & EQUIPMENT—
    HOTEL & RESTAURANT SHEET METAL WORKS INC.
TOBACCO—
    H. RAINVILLE CO. LTD.

The Coffee Mill

TORONTO, ONTARIO (1963–2014)

In the early 1960s, the thought of dining outside by choice was . . . less than cool. For most of Canada, the idea was probably pretty out there, but out went Martha von Heczey, the Hungarian immigrant who had left Budapest after the Second World War, come to Toronto in 1951, and applied for one of the city's first patio licences, for the courtyard of the Lothian Mews. Within a few years, her Yorkville cafe had become an institution, with the stars of the Canadian literati, including Margaret Atwood, George Jonas, along with bohemian

The Coffee Mill in August 1967

beatniks, becoming regular customers and downing cups of espresso on the patio (at the time, it was the only place you could get an espresso besides Cafe Diplomatico, in Little Italy). Big plates of goulash, schnitzel and veal paprikash weighed down the bistro tables underneath fringed umbrellas. When von Heczey moved the cafe to 99 Yorkville in 1974, the regulars followed, and so did the good vibes. She even went so far as to bring along the iconic UNICEF fountain that was at the centre of the mews, getting it out of storage in 1984 and placing it where it still stands today in the Lothian Mews, though the restaurant closed in 2014, much to the dismay of its loyal clientele.

Boston Pizza

CANADA-WIDE (1964–Present)

Gus Agioritis relished his own story: that a Greek merchant marine jumped ship in Canada, opened an Italian restaurant and named it after an American city. Agioritis emigrated from Greece to Canada in 1958 and opened his first restaurant in Edmonton on the corner of 118th Avenue Northwest and 124th Street. The first Boston Pizza and Spaghetti House opened in the summer of 1964, with pizza ovens in the front windows, faux wooden arches, red wallpaper and a stone wall complete with alcoves adorned with small, white Greek statuettes. The menu offered only pizza and pasta, and the former was so foreign to Albertans that when 27-year-old RCMP officer Jim Treliving came in for dinner, he at first didn't know how to eat it. The saving grace was the menu's instructions: "Eat with your hands."

A few years later, Treliving became the restaurant's first franchisee, opening up shop in Penticton, British Columbia in 1968. Five years later he opened two more with co-owner George Melville, and turned Boston Pizza into a household name. When Agioritis founded the restaurant, he was toying with a few names—Santorini Pizza, Acropolis Pizza, Parthenon Pizza—but all those he came up with were already registered. So, why "Boston Pizza"? Well, no one knows for sure. Some say it was because Agioritis found it easy to remember, others say he was a big Bruins fan, so take from that what you will.

Le Roy Jucep

DRUMMONDVILLE, QUEBEC (1964–Present)

The origin story of poutine is complicated. At least three credible stories are accepted in Canadian culinary lore, but the proof is in the curd—or at least in the rights to the intellectual property. Jean-Paul Roy and his wife, Fernande, opened their *casse-croûte*, Le Roy de la Patate, in 1958, returning home to Drummondville after a seven-year stint working in the kitchen at l'hôtel Mont-Royal in Montreal. Little did they know they would go on to create the most recognizable Canadian dish the world over.

Their snack bar did well doling out french fries, gravy and cheese curds, and while Jean-Paul Roy lays claim as being the inventor of poutine, the freshness of those squeaky curds was an important factor in the creation of the messy delight. Thanks to a massive dairy surplus in Quebec during the 1950s, cheese curds were abundant and were commonly sold in snack bars at the front cash. Many people simply tossed them in with their hot french fries. It was Roy's idea to top it all off with gravy.

Six years later, the Roys expanded their business by purchasing the Orange Jucep drive-in and *bar laitier* on Saint-Laurent, where Le Roy Jucep still stands today (not to be confused with the famous Orange Julep in Montreal). While Le Lutin Qui Rit in Warwick, Quebec, also lays claim to inventing poutine, it was Roy who put poutine on the menu for the first time in 1967, after the busy waitresses were complaining about constantly writing out "fries-cheese curds-gravy" on their notepads once the dish became popular. One of the cooks was nicknamed "Ti-pout," and naming the dish poutine was an homage to him.

In 1997, Roy sold Le Roy Jucep to Daniel Leblanc, who then trademarked poutine; the plaque from the Canadian Intellectual Property Office still hangs near the front door. Charles Lambert, the most recent owner since 2011, renovated the interior to bring it back to its drive-in glory days and came upon the tattered recipe for Roy's original sauce. Roy had always claimed it was his gravy that made poutine famous (no doubt influenced by his time working with sauciers in Montreal), and the original recipe is being served once again in Drummondville.

Tim Hortons

CANADA-WIDE (1964–Present)

No restaurant is associated with Canada more than Tim Hortons. Those Dutchies, Double-Doubles and Timbits (b. 1976) are as homey as you can get, and the restaurant has thousands of locations across the country. In every small town, there's a long lineup of cars waiting in the drive-thru for the coffee. But in the early 1960s, hockey player Tim Horton was more interested in the prospect of a fried-chicken and hamburger joint than he was in selling doughnuts. It was a jazz drummer, friend and business partner Jim Charade, who convinced him they could use his hockey star power to sell meals.

In 1963, they opened three Tim Horton Restaurants, offering up a dozen doughnuts for 75 cents, in addition to burgers and fries. Those initial locations were all in Toronto: at 1961 Lawrence Avenue East, 3092 Kingston Road and 111 Lakeshore Boulevard; the fourth was a drive-up burger spot in Port Credit that offered fried-chicken delivery. Like contemporary doughnut shops such as Country Style, or drive-ins like Harvey's, that proliferated in the scene at the time, the restaurants were situated in strip malls or close to well-travelled roads, sometimes inside buildings that formerly housed gas stations in order to attract the carloads of middle-class suburbanites looking for a quick bite.

One of the first Tim Hortons was a burger restaurant—a copycat of the A-frame burger shacks designed by Harvey's—near the Shell service station owned by the Horton family in North Bay, Ontario, known around town as the "Big 7." The first official (the one accepted by the company) Tim Horton's Donuts franchise opened in Hamilton on May 17, 1964, and served only coffee and doughnuts.

The Etymology of a Doughnut Shop

The evolution of the most recognized coffee and doughnut franchise's name is grammatically intriguing. At first, there was Tim Horton's Hamburgers, which served up chicken and burgers. Once the franchise took off, Tim Horton Donuts was the Hamilton original—an interesting choice to not use the Canadian spelling of the round treat, "doughnut." Eventually, "Donuts" was dropped and the shop was known simply as Tim Horton's. In 1993, the company dropped the apostrophe from the spelling, as it was in violation of Quebec's language law, Bill 101. Because the apostrophe is not used in French to show possession, they couldn't use it for the Quebec stores, so opted for "Tim Hortons" for all stores, instead of having two brand names. (And, by the way, "double-double" made its way into the *Canadian Oxford Dictionary* in 2004.)

Restaurant at Barbados and Guyana Pavilion, September 1967

Moskva at Expo 67

MONTREAL, QUEBEC (1967)

More than 150 restaurants at Expo 67 doled out a plentiful buffet of world cuisine that Canadians had never tried before. It lasted for only one year, but their impact can still be seen today. At the much-revered Czechoslovakian pavilion, diners enjoyed appetizers like mousse of ham in cornets, or veal with peaches and almonds baked in a bag, while in the Argentinian pavilion, guests enjoyed huge steaks, fine cheeses and Argentinian wines at the 428-seat El Gaucho. One of the restaurants most talked about was Moskva, in the Russian pavilion, for many reasons, including how Russia would have looked to the outside world at this point. The media talked incessantly about their "capitalistic prices" (vodka shots for $1.50).

The Moskva dining room was large and rectangular, with a black-and-white mural of Red Square, and tables organized in long straight lines. With eleven hundred seats, Moskva was by far the largest dining experience at the expo, with a few different dining halls, a banquet hall, cafeteria and food bar selling hundreds of dishes—everything from borscht and fuchka soups, shashlik and smoked salmon, to beluga caviar from the Caspian Sea (ringing in at $2.25 for a small spoonful), Crimean champagne, and haze grouse in melted butter, not to mention a new-to-Canadians dish called chicken Kiev, which spurted with butter when sliced into.

The Naam

VANCOUVER, BRITISH COLUMBIA (1968–Present)

In the 1960s, hippies followed the "Rainbow Road," aka West 4th Avenue, to Kitsilano; thanks to city rezoning, which made boarding houses affordable, and its proximity to the beach, this area became a counterculture hot spot. As Vancouver filled up with American conscientious objectors to the Vietnam War and hippies exploring Eastern philosophy, a cook from the popular Golden Lotus Natural Food, which had opened as the city's first vegetarian restaurant, opened The Naam just down the block, operating it as a collective and offering up a natural food store and vegetarian restaurant. It soon became a hub of the counterculture.

Peter Keith and Bob Woodsworth bought The Naam in 1981, and it remains on West 4th Avenue today, among the natural food stores and yoga studios. The menu does have some new plant-based options, like vegan cheese and eggs, but foundationally it consists of many of the same options as when it first opened: scrambled tofu with vegetables, and buckwheat pancakes with bananas for brunch; dragon bowls with steamed vegetables and curry, or veggie nut patties for dinner.

Naam Natural Foods Restaurant, October 1974

Mary Brown's

ST. JOHN'S, NEWFOUNDLAND AND LABRADOR
(1969–Present)

Mary Brown's, as it's known today, used to be called Golden Skillet. Pat Tarrant and Cyril Fleming saw an ad in the *Montreal Gazette* for a franchising opportunity for the Richmond, Virginia–based chain and jumped at the chance to bring fried chicken to Newfoundland and Labrador. They opened their first location in the Avalon Mall in 1969, well before there was a food court there, or anywhere in Canada, for that matter. A snack pack, with two pieces of fried chicken, fries and a roll, cost 95 cents, and you could add coleslaw for 20 cents more. Before they knew it, they needed to rebrand because of copyright issues and so became Mary Brown's Fried Chicken, named after the wife of the Golden Skillet's founder. Now the Big Mary fans and tater devotees (which didn't make the menu until the 1980s) are Canada-wide, with locations in places where Newfoundland transplant communities are strong, like Fort McMurray, Alberta.

CHAPTER NINE

The 1970s

"George Tidball took a chance. . . . The rest is part of wilted lettuce history."

The salad bar. This veritable vegetable parade of chopped iceberg lettuce, shredded carrots and cherry tomatoes, plus the inevitable ranch dressing, sits at a standstill, chilled in the stainless-steel bins filled with ice. It's now so ingrained in Canadian steakhouse culture it's almost cliché, but before the 1970s, it didn't exist. When George Tidball first opened The Keg in an old industrial building in North Vancouver in 1971, he took a chance on a trend he had seen in American restaurants. The rest is part of wilted lettuce history.

Along with economic upheaval, and the October Crisis and martial law in Quebec, the 1970s saw a new wave of counterculture dining, with vegetarian restaurants and feminist coffee houses serving up health-conscious and organic dishes across the country. With the increase of women in the workforce, takeout became more popular than ever for busy families. The number of Indian restaurants increased, and Edo brought Japanese Teppanyaki to the suburbs. The year the salad bar was tossed onto the dining scene was also the first time in the country's history that the majority of immigrants arriving in Canada were not of European ancestry, meaning the options for dining out were ever-expanding as the concept of multiculturalism cemented itself onto the plate.

Along with an increase in the variety of cuisines, restaurants grew physically (and deliciously) larger as they became entrenched in the entertainment industry; they became a part of the society's lifestyle, and the idea of the restaurant as entertainment came into its own. This was a decade of major decor moves, with stained glass, mirrored walls, barber chairs at the bar and the establishment of themed restaurants as an institution.

Houston Pizza

REGINA, SASKATCHEWAN (1970–Present)

Across Canada, there is a surprising number of regional varieties when it comes to pizza. Every local spot has its twist. In Pictou County, Nova Scotia, the sauce is a dark brown and always topped with Brothers pepperoni; in Windsor, Ontario, it's all about the matchstick pepperoni. A common thread? They were created by Greeks, as was the Regina-style pie, which entered the Canadian culinary canon in 1970. Houston Pizza was started by John Kolitsas (who immigrated to Canada

in 1963 at the age of 22 from Andros, Greece) and his three brothers, George, Tony and Gus.

They started slinging daily special pizzas, selling them for 99 cents each out of the Kitchener Hotel on Rose Street in May 1970, before moving to their landmark location on Hill Avenue in September of the same year. They quickly gained popularity for their unique style of pizza, which has been duplicated so many times it's now known as Regina-style pizza. The owners of Western Pizza are first cousins, and many of the chefs of other pizza spots passed through the kitchen on Hill Avenue before opening their own shops.

Houston's all-dressed is a tall order, literally. The nine toppings on the Traditional All Dressed are piled high— like, several inches of deli meats high— the green pepper, mushroom and onion wedged between a thick pizza crust and a thick layer of browned cheese. Served up in a deep pan, Houston's pizza is cut into squares because of all the toppings, and some people eat the slices with their two hands, like a sandwich, or choose to eat with a knife and fork. Only one question is to be asked about this Prairie deep-dish pie: Are you a centre-piece person or an outside-piece person?

Indian Rice Factory

TORONTO, ONTARIO (1970–2013)

A béchamel sauce yellowed with curry powder was the catalyst for the opening of one of Toronto's first Indian restaurants. There were only two Indian restaurants in the city when Amar Patel, a nurse from Bombay, dined at the Cafe l'Auberge at the Inn on the Park Hotel at Eglinton and Leslie. She was mortified by the Indian chafing dishes, the chicken, beef and shrimp bathing in a mess of bécha-mel with curry powder. Patel called up

the manager, and then went to work for the chef at the hotel after cooking him a meal filled with authentic Indian dishes.

Patel opened her own restaurant on Dupont Street in 1970, the Indian Rice Factory. Patel's restaurant is said to also be the catalyst for the love affair Toronto has with Indian food. Three years after she opened on Dupont, there were only 15 Indian eateries in the city; today there are hundreds.

Alycia's

WINNIPEG, MANITOBA (1971–2011)

It always smelled of fried onions at Alycia's. When her husband died in 1971, Marion Staff took over Alice's, a 20-seat restaurant on the corner of Cathedral Avenue and McGregor Street because cooking was all she knew how to do. Staff had only a sixth-grade education, but growing up with seven brothers on a farm in rural Winnipeg, she had learned to cook at an early age and loved it. She leaned into her Ukrainian heritage, renaming the restaurant Alycia's in 1977, and began serving up thousands of perogies a day and growing the small restaurant into a cornerstone of Winnipeg's North End dining scene. Mismatched tables were covered in linens adorned with Ukrainian needlework, plastic covers protecting them from the bowls full of borscht. Rye bread, kielbasa, vinegary coleslaw, cabbage rolls and, of course, the quintessential Ukrainian dish, potato and cheddar perogies—the food earned Alycia's the honour of being actor John Candy's favourite restaurant.

Gourmet Fair at Sherway Gardens circa 1979

Gourmet Fare
at Sherway Gardens

ETOBICOKE, ONTARIO (1971–Present)

Landscape architect George Tanaka designed the Sherway Gardens shopping centre to include several garden-like courtyards, offering up a climate-controlled Zen-hopeful shopping experience. And the choice of food there? Well, early shopping malls had one, maybe two restaurants, separated from the shopping space as their own entity. Enter the mall food court.

The Rouse Company, founded by James W. Rouse, who is credited with coining the term "shopping mall," was building Sherway Gardens when the team brainstormed with businessman and architect consultant Gordon Peck on the creation of an indoor version of a food market, or "community picnics," inspired by those popular in Beverly Hills at the time. The company had requested restaurant stalls, with a fence in front of them, but Peck didn't like that—what if he wanted to eat Chinese food and his wife wanted Italian? They wouldn't be able to eat together. So, the

16 restaurants stalls at Gourmet Fair at Sherway Gardens made up the first food court in North America, known back then as a "food cluster," with all independent shops, such as the Cookie Man, which offered up coffee and a cookie for 30 cents, and the guy selling fresh popcorn from a faux carnival cart. Located on the lower level, it was really was fair-like, with colourful flags hanging from the ceiling, cube stools and a faux gold ashtray on every table.

The mall food court became a community meeting point for many; some had their first taste of Mexican food, or borscht from Ukrainian Caravan Foods there. Kids would hustle over to Sherway Gardens after school, crowding those stools at one tile-topped table as they downed frozen Cokes, taters and cheesecake, the smell of fresh baking and cigarette smoke lingering in the air. In the mid-2010s, the food court moved upstairs and became Gourmet Fare, part of the mall's $550-million renovation.

Fat Frank's

HALIFAX, NOVA SCOTIA (1973–late 1980s)

When famed *New York Times* columnist Craig Claiborne came to Halifax in the spring of 1976, he was expecting a rinky-dink tundra of a town. Instead, he praised two notable restaurants: Five Fisherman, which still stands today as one of the best in the city (albeit in one of Halifax's most haunted buildings), and Fat Frank's. He complimented the nice oil paintings on the wall of "the most elegant of Halifax's restaurants" and described the menu—beginning with snails and mushrooms on toast, and smoked salmon, and then moving on to veal cordon bleu, turtle steak with a caper and paprika sauce, and sweetbreads with ham—as being "fascinating and well-executed."

Fat Frank, otherwise known as Frank Metzger, from Cleveland, opened Fat Frank's Very Small Restaurant on Argyle Street in 1973, and very small it was. Measuring only seven feet wide, the restaurant had little space between the six tables that almost touched (no secrets between diners, that's for sure). It was so small, in fact, that it didn't qualify for a liquor licence, so those who knew Frank could ask for a Chinese tea, red or white, to get a glass of vintage French wine.

The self-described "Edwardian dining" restaurant raved about by Claiborne moved to Spring Garden Road in 1974, where Haligonians celebrated anniversaries, prom nights and other special occasions for more than a decade, enchanted by bottles of Château Margaux, escargots, and bouillabaisse.

"Fat Frank" Metzger, 30, serves *Toronto Star* travel editor Gerry Hall in his restaurant, 1973

Afghan Horsemen

VANCOUVER, BRITISH COLUMBIA (1974–Present)

Afghan food may not be as ubiquitous in Canada as sushi or pizza, but it has a coast-to-coast presence, and Afghan Horsemen in Vancouver was one of the first places to serve it. Zaher Nasiri came to Canada from Afghanistan in 1970, almost a decade before his home country was invaded by the Soviets, causing a big influx of immigrants from that country. He opened the Afghan Horsemen just off Granville Island with his wife, Razia Nasiri, in 1974, offering up a few dishes from his home country, and warming up doubtful patrons with Mediterranean favourites like hummus and lamb kebabs. But he soon also started offering up authentic bolani and mantu.

Now, almost five decades later Afghan Horsemen is still busy as ever, serving huge trays of grilled lamp chops and beef shish kebab lined with pakawra, thiny sliced battered and fried potatoes. Afghan tapestries decorate the walls, and old photography, framed drawings, and ornate rugs line virtually every surface of the restaurant, save for one mural of Afghan horsemen galloping across the wall.

Silver Inn Restaurant

CALGARY, ALBERTA (1975–2022)

For the mother of ginger beef, it was all about keeping it in the family. Kwai Sin Sheung wanted to ensure her six children were all in one place, and the best way she knew how was to open a restaurant. There were no Peking-style restaurants in Calgary in the 1970s, and she felt it would be a good fit, as Calgary and the Beijing region are of similar latitude, both with meat- and starch-heavy diets. So, after luring two of her daughters back from England, where they had first emigrated from Hong Kong, sisters Louise Tsang and Lily Wong, along with her husband George Wong, opened

the Silver Inn Restaurant in 1975 at 4th Street Southwest. They moved the restaurant to its current location at 2702 Centre Street North in 1978.

Their dish no. 65, the "deep fried shredded beef in chili sauce," is known across the Prairies by those who love it as "ginger beef." Those deep-fried strips of beef coated in a sticky vinegary-garlicky-gingery sauce and tossed with julienned carrots and onions is on most menus in any small-town Chinese restaurant and is as ubiquitous as chicken balls.

George Wong, the restaurant's chef, was working on some new menu items to entice white diners (who made up most of their patronage) and felt that the Peking-style beef wouldn't appeal to his customers—he thought that locals would like something deep-fried and with gravy (he had, after all, spent time working in kitchens in Britain and was well acquainted with the Brits' love affair with gravy). So, into the deep fryer that Alberta beef went, before being coated in sweet chili-ginger sauce. But because most people couldn't seem to remember what No. 65 was called (often mistaking the pepperiness of ginger in other dishes for spicy heat that was really the chilies), when ordering they would ask for "the beef with the ginger stuff"—and ginger beef, Calgary-style, was born. The owners of the Silver Inn helped create an iconic dish in Calgary that has surely brought many intrepid food pilgrims through the doors, but for the Cheung family it wasn't about making lots of money, it was about having their family all together. Their brother Kwong Cheung ran the restaurant until his retirement in October 2022. At the Silver Inn in Calgary, the dish was always just "no. 65."

Ginger Beef

Recipe inspired by
The Silver Inn

Kwong Cheung spoke to me over the phone about the importance of using tender beef when making ginger beef. And although he wouldn't give up the Silver Inn's exact recipe, like most dishes in Alberta, this recipe is all about the beef. To keep it tender, even after deep-frying, slice it thinly against the grain.

1. Slice the beef against the grain into ½-inch (1.2 cm) long strips.

2. Heat the oil in a deep pot or wok over medium-high heat.

3. Combine the egg, cornstarch, flour, white pepper and 1 cup (250 ml) water in a large bowl. Toss the beef in the batter to coat.

4. Fry the beef in the oil, about five strips at a time, until golden and crispy, about 3 minutes. Set the fried beef aside on a plate lined with paper towel to drain while you cook the remaining beef strips. Make sure to let the oil come back up to temperature in between batches.

5. To make the sauce, whisk together the sugar, soy sauces, rice wine vinegar, Chinese cooking wine and chilies with ½ cup (125 ml) water in a small bowl.

SERVES 4 TO 6

1 pound (450 g) flank steak

2 to 3 cups (500 to 750 ml) vegetable oil, for frying

Rice, for serving

Batter

1 egg

1¼ cups (310 ml) cornstarch

3 Tbsp (45 ml) all-purpose flour

1½ tsp (7 ml) ground white pepper

1 cup (250 ml) water

Sauce

¼ cup (60 ml) granulated sugar (or ½ cup/125 ml, if you like it sweet)

¼ cup (60 ml) soy sauce

3 Tbsp (45 ml) dark soy sauce

2 Tbsp (30 ml) rice wine vinegar

2 Tbsp (30 ml) Chinese cooking wine

1½ tsp (7 ml) crushed chilies, plus extra to taste

½ cup (125 ml) water

6. In the wok, stir-fry carrot and bell peppers with the garlic and ginger over medium-high heat until crispy. Add the sauce and bring to a boil, cooking until it thickens.

7. Add the beef to the vegetable mixture, stirring well. Serve immediately with rice.

Vegetables

1 large carrot, julienned

1 red bell pepper, julienned

1 green bell pepper, julienned

6 cloves garlic, thinly sliced

2 Tbsp (30 ml) minced ginger

Richard's Fresh Seafood

COVEHEAD, PRINCE EDWARD ISLAND (1976–Present)

"Taste the ocean" doesn't quite qualify the experience of sitting on the patio outside Richard's Fresh Seafood shack; you can smell the salty air, feel the wind whipping against you, see that iconic red earth and taste their famous lobster rolls. And those lobster rolls are perfect, with pink plump claws mixed in a lemony mayo with chopped celery and chives, then encased in a long, lightly toasted bun. The fish and chips and scallop burgers are also a major draw here, but when Richard Watts first opened his snack bar, in 1976, there was no seafood whatsoever on the menu.

He started with burgers and fries, along with other deep-fried foods that could be found in any snack bar across the country at the time. But Watts also ran Richard's deep-sea fishing tours out of Covehead Harbour, and eventually he started serving up fresh catch on the daily. It is now one of the most popular seafood shacks on the Island, with a lineup that forms well before opening time and flows until closing.

Ryan Doucet took over the seafood shop in 2010, and in 2019 opened a second location in Victoria-by-the-Sea, which is just as popular.

King of Donair

HALIFAX, NOVA SCOTIA (1977–Present)

It's 3 a.m. on a hot September night (well, morning, really) at a downtown intersection known as Pizza Corner and there is a lineup out the door at King of Donair. University students have poured themselves out of the bars to dine while sitting on the curb, eating Halifax's most iconic food. Donair is the drunk food that became a city icon.

Peter Gamoulakos left the small town of Levetsovo in Greece in 1959, landing in Halifax, and he spent the 1970s furiously opening restaurants. The first was one of the early pizza shops in the city, Velos Pizza, followed by Velos Souvlakia Sunnyside in Bedford in partnership with his brother-in-law Peter Dikaios and brother George Gamoulakos, in 1973. This is where the donair's history begins.

Like the Chinese restaurateurs who added sugar to their traditional dishes to cater to the North American sweet tooth, Gamoulakos altered the recipe for doner kebab, the iconic Turkish street food he'd fallen in love with while on a trip home to Greece, in order to tantalize Haligonians. He substituted the doner's usual lamb for more commonplace beef and made his own version of tzatziki by swapping out the yogurt for evaporated milk and adding sugar—at one point, he even advertised the donair as being covered in cheese sauce to entice locals who would have found the garlicky Greek condiment a tad too foreign.

It wasn't until 1976, when Peter and his brother John Kamoulakos (their last names are different because of an immigration kerfuffle) opened Mr. Donair on Quinpool Road, that the donair took off in Halifax. The rebranding to King of Donair in 1977 said it all; there were now donair shops across the city and it quickly became a favourite food.

While ownership of the restaurant has changed several times, the donair's impact on the dining scene across Canada is evident. There are eight King of Donair locations, including one in Saskatoon, three in Alberta, and others serving up Maritime-style donairs across the country, but many people still make the pilgrimage to Halifax to sample the real thing.

In the 1990s, King of Donair (a.k.a. KOD) opened a location on the iconic Pizza Corner intersection of Grafton and Blowers Streets, cementing the wrap into the ethos of late-late-night dining in Halifax. The Pizza Corner KOD location closed in 2012 because of a rental dispute, but the donair lives on at Johnny K's, the name a tribute to its inventor, opened in 2015 at the same location.

These days, everyone from your grandma to Anthony Bourdain has taken a bite, and there are chefs across the country doing high-end versions of this late-night feed (Donair steamed buns, anyone?). In 2015, the donair was chosen as Halifax's official food.

East Coast Donair Sauce

Recipe inspired by
King of Donair

One of the defining characteristics of a Halifax donair is the sauce—a sweet, tangy elixir that East Coasters love on their donairs, on their pizza and on their garlic fingers ... and on a whole lot of other things too these days. Donair sauce as a condiment is fair game on menus across the Maritimes—you'll find it on everything from steamed buns to cheesecake (yup, that's right, the Sweet Hereafter in Halifax had a donair cheesecake). Garlic fingers, simply a pizza pie piled high with mozzarella and garlic cut into strips, is another much-beloved Atlantic Canadian invention, and donair sauce for dunking is a requirement for this dish. There's also one incredibly controversial ingredient that pizza-shop owners and eaters have debated for generations: To garlic powder or to not garlic powder?

**MAKES ABOUT
1½ CUPS (375 ML)**

⅔ cup (160 ml) evaporated milk

⅔ cup (160 ml) granulated sugar

½ tsp (2 ml) garlic powder (controversially optional)

¼ cup (60 ml) white vinegar

1. In a large bowl, mix together the evaporated milk and sugar until the sugar is dissolved. If using the garlic powder, add it and mix until well incorporated.

2. Slowly drizzle in the vinegar, folding it into the mixture. Do not stir too aggressively or whisk, or the sauce will split and clump.

3. Transfer the sauce to a glass container and refrigerate, sealed, for at least 1 hour before serving.

Kensington Patty Palace

TORONTO, ONTARIO (1977–Present)

Hearing the crackle of the waxed-paper envelope and smelling the aroma of curried beef as you bite into a hot yellow patty is a quintessential Toronto experience. The Jamaican patty is ubiquitous throughout the city. It was derived from the Cornish pasty, a baked pastry filled with meat or vegetables brought to the Caribbean by British colonists in the 17th century, made delicious by the enslaved African people who were shipped to the Caribbean and by the Indian and Chinese people who had been brought as indentured workers.

In Toronto, you can grab a patty on your way down into the subway system, at a gas station or at a convenience store, but they were nearly destroyed in the mid-1980s. When Raymond and Pat Davidson, and their son, Michael, opened their Kensington Market Jamaican bakery on Baldwin Street in 1977, after leaving their home country (among the thousands who emigrated from the Caribbean to Canada in the 1960s and 1970s), which was rife with politically incited violence, they had no idea of the fight they were in for.

A visit from Consumer and Corporate Affairs grew into what is known as the Toronto Patty Wars of February 1985 when the federal inspectors realized that the "beef patty" didn't align with the Meat Inspection Act's definition (a "beef patty" could consist only of meat and seasoning you would put in a hamburger).

Each facing a hefty fine of $5,000, the Davidsons and owners of other patty shops protested their notices, and so did the city that loved its baked goods. After a week of media scrutiny, public outcry and a snack stop by the Ontario Opposition leader David Peterson, the government relented, and the city continued to love what could be considered one of its signature dishes: the spicy beef patty.

The Davidsons have since departed Kensington Market, setting up their patty-making plant in Scarborough, but there's still the Golden Patty on Baldwin to scratch that itch. Or you can find a patty at one the dozens of spots throughout the city. After all, the city even has day dedicated to the beloved baked good: February 23 is Toronto's Patty Day.

Mitzi's Chicken Finger Restaurant

WINNIPEG, MANITOBA (1978–Present)

To those adults who still order chicken fingers every time they go out to eat: you're not alone. In its heyday, dozens of people lined up outside Mitzi's Chicken Finger Restaurant in Winnipeg to devour the famous chicken fingers with the super-secret honey-dill dipping sauce. Shirley Eng emigrated from Hong Kong in the early 1970s and with her husband, Peter (who was born in China but educated in Hong Kong), she bought an existing restaurant, which they turned into Mitzi's.

For the first decade, they served up Chinese-Canadian classics and business was okay, but in 1988 they closed for a few months to revamp the menu. That's when Peter decided they should go all in on the chicken finger. More than 30 years later, their pink-stuccoed building is still one of the most beloved in the city. Legend has it that the super-secret, super-successful sauce Peter created is actually a copycat of another restaurant's sauce, but either way, it's a happy accident that it became a Manitoban classic.

Le Saint-Amour

QUEBEC CITY, QUEBEC (1978–Present)

An inconspicuous entrance on the rue Sainte-Ursule in Quebec City's Old Town leads to a majorly romantic greenhouse-like dining room with white tablecloths and French cuisine that has shifted the way we look at local food in Quebec. Chef Jean-Luc Boulay emigrated from France in 1976 with an arsenal of French cooking skills to work in Montreal during the Olympic Games, and it was his perfect omelette that settled his culinary fate. While working in Quebec City post-Olympics, the 24-year-old answered an ad for head chef of a new restaurant, and after wowing Jacques Fortier with the best omelette of his life, the two opened Le Saint-Amour in 1978.

From the beginning, the restaurant has been staunchly French in its technique but uses local Quebec ingredients and unconventional twists to create a gastronomical shift that still creates aftershocks in this country. The chef's brigade has churned out amazing, award-winning chefs (Boulay still instructs the apprentices to prepare the foie gras twice a week), and the restaurant to this day is beloved for its cream of cucumber potage, Charlevoix veal, lobster terrines and sous-vide foie gras, not to mention the twelve-thousand-bottle wine cellar featuring at least a thousand French wines.

Korean Village Restaurant

TORONTO, ONTARIO (1978–Present)

When Jason Lee was growing up, he wasn't interested at all in the family business, or his culture. His mother, Ok Re Lee, an actress, and his father, Ke Hang Lee, a fitness teacher, moved with him to Toronto from Seoul in the late 1970s, when he was only three months old. The couple, who couldn't speak English, opted to open a Korean restaurant, even though they had zero formal industry experience. Korean Village Restaurant opened in 1978, one of the first Korean businesses at Bloor and Christie, which at that time was transitioning into Toronto's Koreatown. In the late 1960s, there were only about a hundred Koreans in Toronto, but by the time the restaurant opened, there were ten thousand, thanks to the shifts in the Immigration Act of 1967 and the introduction of the point system, an evaluation method in which immigrants were assigned points in different categories, related to how well they would settle in Canada.

A tumultuous childhood led to Jason getting kicked out of the house, but when his dad got sick, Jason returned to Koreatown and started managing the restaurant, finally learned how to speak Korean—and falling in love with the restaurant. In 2006, when he took over as general manager, he pared the menu down from over 250 items to 35 and championed the success of the restaurant and his community. Now, Lee is an active member of the Koreatown BIA and even gives tours of the neighbourhood when he's not at the restaurant. The matriarch came into the restaurant every day, spending two hours getting ready for her shift (looking glamorous continued to be of great importance to her), until she died in 2019.

The family restaurant is still going strong through the pandemic, offering sizzling bibimbap, savoury bulgogi and mountains of japchae, served with lots of banchan and kimchi—all devoured daily at this Bloor Street West institution.

Top: Owner Jason Lee
with his mother,
Ok Re Lee

Cedar's Eatery

CHARLOTTETOWN, PRINCE EDWARD ISLAND
(1979–Present)

Fouad "Freddie" Yammine opened Cedar's Eatery at 81 University Avenue in 1979 with a pretty run-of-the-mill menu: burgers and fries. His sister, Nawal Abdallah (who came to Prince Edward Island in the late 1970s from Lebanon, where she had worked as a secretary) took over the restaurant soon after, along with her husband Maroun Abdallah.

For decades, the family served only a few Lebanese dishes; between the fact that most Islanders were meat-and-potatoes people and that they had to import all their Middle Eastern ingredients (the local grocery stores didn't even sell olive oil in the early 1980s. As for chickpeas, tahini, and grape leaves? Forget about it!), the most ordered dishes on the menu were hamburgers; falafel didn't even make an appearance until the early 2000s. But it was the garlic sauce (known as toum) on the chicken that kept people coming back and coaxed hesitant Charlottetown diners into ordering more Lebanese fare. That garlic sauce became so popular that the Abdallahs' son, Ryan, focused on merchandising after taking over the business in 2010. Eventually, in 2017, the Original Maroun's Garlic Spread started being sold in Sobeys Atlantic Canada locations.

In 1991, Yammine and the Abdallahs opened Baba's upstairs. The lounge features live music, and on a Friday or Saturday night, you can hear the university students partying and dancing to the beat of the music as the sound carries through the ceilings into the restaurant's dining room.

"The local grocery stores didn't even sell olive oil in the early 1980s."

CHAPTER TEN

The 1980s

"Another trend helped bring the nation together: the rise of chain restaurants."

Tim Hortons, Harvey's, Dairy Queen, McDonald's, A&W. By the 1980s, driving the main drags of the country, from Vancouver to St. John's, meant you would have seen the same five soaring, incredibly well-lit, signs for the same five chains. Fast-food chains were more popular than ever—in the mid-1980s, restaurant sales in Canada brought in over $12 billion a year; just 20 years earlier it was less than $800 million. In the decade in which Canada adopted its constitution, another trend helped bring the nation, which was suffering a crisis of community, together: the rise of chain restaurants.

Dual-income families ate out regularly and yuppies had no qualms about slapping splashy suppers on their credit cards as dining out became higher end than ever before. It became a status symbol to eat at the hottest new restaurants. As conspicuous consumption became the norm, chefs themselves became well known, and the persnickety voices of local restaurant critics in the newspaper got louder. Nouvelle cuisine trends from the United States highlighted the pulled-back nature of high-end dining with clean, crisp flavours, while Asia's cuisine established itself in the mainstream, with countless Vietnamese, Japanese and Thai restaurants opening across the country. Tex-Mex restaurants also became abundant, and another soaring sign hit the main drag: *bienvenidos* Taco Bell.

L'Express

MONTREAL, QUEBEC (1980–Present)

The bustling sounds of L'Express could almost be a soundtrack of a Parisian restaurant in a movie. Laughter and vivacious conversations ping off the mirrored walls as waiters in long white aprons squeeze between the tables for two, rushing across the checkerboard floor. Chicken liver pâté, sorrel soup, confit duck leg, steak tartare and plates of homemade ravioli are enjoyed at the white tableclothed tables after the requisite baguette, jar of cornichons and pot of mustard are cleared away. L'Express is the dream of Colette Brossoit and Pierre Villeneuve; it opened in 1980 on the main floor of a three-storey stone house on rue Saint-Denis, its owners motivated to offer something more casual and accessible than the stuffy French fine dining prevalent in Montreal at the time.

At first, L'Express featured a nondescript menu of sandwiches. Enter French chef Joël Chapoulie, who moved from France after Expo 67 and in 1982 transformed the menu to what it is today. It hasn't changed much since. For more than 40 years, L'Express has been offering breakfast, lunch and dinner (until really late, to support local artists' post-show schedules); it is quintessentially French but unequivocally Québécois.

Happy Garden Restaurant

EDMONTON, ALBERTA (1980–2018)

Edmonton loves green-onion cakes (or scallion pancakes, as they're more commonly known in North America). They are everywhere in its restaurants, not just at Chinese spots: these savoury hotcakes are found in Vietnamese eateries, Irish pubs and even at a green-onion pancake–themed food truck. And it's all because of one man, Siu To. He emigrated from China in 1978 and two years later opened up Happy Garden Restaurant in the Edmonton neighbourhood of Parkallen, serving up Chinese staples, but his green-onion cakes, which were new to the city, were his most popular appetizer.

To began taking the flaky, pan-fried onion cakes to Edmonton's big festivals (they were there at the beginning of the Fringe), convinced their enticing aromas would lure more trepidatious diners to his stand, and they made out like gangbusters—they became *the* thing to eat at the festivals.

Happy Garden closed in 2018, but To has since opened the Green Onion Cake Man, focusing on pumping out the pancakes on the regular.

BeaverTails

OTTAWA, ONTARIO (1980–Present)

It's not surprising that in a cold-weather country, a fresh hot pastry is one of Canada's most recognizable foods, named after Canada's most iconic animal. The BeaverTails pastry is a fried treat consisting of whole-wheat dough pulled pre-frying by hand to resemble the long, flat tail of a beaver. Grant and Pam Hooker got their start at the Killaloe Craft and Community Fair in the late 1970s, where they started selling breakfast pastries for a dollar, using Grant's German grandmother's recipe. But it wasn't until their daughter remarked how much the pastry looked like a beaver tail that they knew how they would market it.

They opened the very first BeaverTails store in ByWard Market in 1980 to some success, but it was when they opened their riverside stand on the Rideau Canal that the doughnut-bannock baby entered the Canadian culinary canon. The classic is dusted with cinnamon and sugar—or try the Killaloe Sunrise, with its added lemon, or the Hazel Amour, slathered with a thick layer of chocolate hazelnut spread.

Top: BeaverTails at the Rideau Canal in 1981

MJ's Kafé

STEINBACH, MANITOBA (1981–Present)

It's noon at MJ's Kafé and the place is packed with families, regulars, out-of-towners and women wearing Mennonite bonnets. And it's been like that for decades. The Steinbach restaurant serving traditional Mennonite cuisine opened in 1981, but it was when Bryan Bartel and his mother, Margaret, took over the place in 1988 that the schmauntfat really got cooking. Thousands of Russian Mennonites came to Winnipeg in the late 1870s and 1880s, bringing with them a rich culinary tradition and Low German dialect, both of which MJ's serves in spades to the hungry residents of Steinbach, a mostly Mennonite community. You'll find big plates of varenyky (the Russian cousin to Ukrainian perogies but double the size) covered with onions fried in bacon fat and topped with schmauntfat, a creamy rich gravy (Bryan estimates they use about 1,200 pounds of butter and 500 gallons of cream per year making it), served with schinkjefleesch, or farmer sausage. There's also borscht and kielke, not to mention Canadian favourites like burgers, fries and Manitoba fried pickerel. Oh, bay yo! As they say at MJ's.

Lang's Cafe

REGINA, SASKATCHEWAN (1982–2018)

If you eat Vietnamese food in Regina, there's a pretty good chance it will be made by someone in the Tran family. In the decade after the Vietnam War, which ended in 1975, over a hundred thousand Vietnamese immigrated to Canada. Only three thousand of these immigrants, known as "boat people," ended up in Saskatchewan, including Minh Van Tran who, along with his father, Lang Tran, opened one of the first Vietnamese restaurants in the country—Lang's Cafe— in Regina in 1982.

Lang and Minh had arrived with their spouses, Minh's 3 children and 10 of his siblings. The siblings went on to start more than 10 restaurants between them— 5 in Regina and several in Vancouver, including the popular Lunch Lady, owned by Victoria Tran (her son Michael opened the Pacific Poke chain in 2016).

The family arrived in Yorkton in 1979 but, after experiencing racism, left within a year for Regina. Lang's Cafe on Broad Street became a landmark restaurant in the city, known for the pho, spring rolls, fresh rolls and noodle dishes. Sadly, it was destroyed by fire in 2018.

Marché Méli-Mélo Caraibe

MONTREAL, QUEBEC (1984–Present)

Montreal's *épiceries* are treasure troves of entrees from all over the world, their lunch counters and shelves laden with dishes (many pre-packaged in Styrofoam) for you to enjoy. And, like all the best places, Marché Méli-Mélo Caraibe is unassuming on the outside. DHL placards are plastered all over the windows, bags of beans are stacked high in the windows next to a bin of wooden spoons. Jean-Michel Baptiste emigrated from Haiti in the early 1980s and opened this Afro-Caribbean market with friend Jean-Marie Toussain.

Inside, at the back counter past the canned goods, fresh veg and beauty products from the Caribbean and Africa, there is a taste of Haiti that can be found nowhere else in Montreal. Pork griot and beef tasso come with mountains of rice and beans and fried plantain. In 2017, Baptiste and Toussain also opened a full-fledged eatery called Méli-Mélo Le Néo Resto on Bélanger, which has 60 seats and full lunch and dinner menus, with dishes like sweet plantains croquettes with avocado cream, soup joumou and lalo.

Bishop's

VANCOUVER, BRITISH COLUMBIA (1985–2022)

Bishop's felt old school with its white linens, dim lighting and antique silverware, but it was new wave since, well, it was new. John Bishop opened his self-titled restaurant in 1985 on West 4th Avenue in Kitsilano after parting ways with Umberto Menghi at Giardino, one of Vancouver's most iconic restaurants.

Born in Wales, Bishop came to Canada in 1973 and shifted the Canadian perspective on fine dining, which until then had always meant French. He helped create West Coast farm-to-table cooking that set the standard for contemporary BC cuisine by cultivating relationships with local producers and fisher people. He made local high-end in Vancouver, and it has become a classic restaurant that has churned out dozens of influential Canadian chefs, like Rob Feenie and Jeff Van Geest. Despite 2020 promises to its regular diners to reopen post-pandemic, the iconic restaurant closed for good in early 2022, blaming an exorbitant rent increase.

Gasthof Old Bavarian Restaurant

SUSSEX, NEW BRUNSWICK (1985–Present)

If you take a wrong turn on Route 890 near Sussex, you might think you've ended up in southern Germany. The Gasthof Old Bavarian Restaurant's sheep graze on the hill behind the alpine guesthouse, its second-floor balcony lined with red flowers. The Giermindl family—Adolph, Olga and their 11 children—arrived in Canada from Germany in 1976 with their sights set on buying a farm. They purchased a property in Sussex, New Brunswick, because it reminded them of the rolling hills of Bavaria, and Adolph's butcher shop opened a year later, though that wasn't in the original plan. Adolph had butchered a moose for someone as a favour, and they told him he just had to open a butcher shop, but operating a farm-to-table restaurant was his dream.

In 1985, the Gasthof Old Bavarian Restaurant opened its doors, outfitted with low wooden booths and blue gingham tablecloths. Tall pint glasses of Erdinger pair with the huge plates of traditional German food such as roast pork hocks, sauerkraut and potato salad. All the meats on the menu, from the veal bratwurst to the pork schnitzel, come from the farm. Even the livestock eats well: they are fed from grain grown on the farm. These days, three of the daughters run the business: Maria runs the farm, Inge runs the butcher shop and Claudia manages the restaurant, welcoming like family everyone who ends up on the farm.

Lotus

TORONTO, ONTARIO (1987–1997)

The combination of ingredients and techniques from east and west are what put Susur Lee's first restaurant, Lotus, on the map when he opened the 16-table restaurant on Tecumseh Street in 1987. Lee created a new sort of fusion that

mixed his experience in Hong Kong with his French training and hit the Canadian dining scene by storm. The international critics soon came. When *New York Times* writer Nancy Harmon Jenkins visited Toronto in 1994, hailing it as a multicultural culinary wonderland, she said of Lee: "When critics talk of fusion cooking, surely this is what they mean—a chef whose palate was formed in Asia but who has a sure grasp of European ingredients and techniques," this after dining on translucently-thin sashimi paired with a Vidalia onion salad, and seared tuna topped with citrus crème fraîche. His Singapore slaw was one of the most famous examples of the fusion cuisine at Susur, the restaurant he opened after Lotus, and now at Lee.

Tojo's

VANCOUVER, BRITISH COLUMBIA (1988–Present)

Hidekazu Tojo learned how to roll with it. When the Japanese chef arrived in Vancouver in 1971 after apprenticing in Osaka, sushi was not widespread; there were fewer than five Japanese restaurants in the city, and scarcely anyone liked to eat sushi, fearful of raw fish and seaweed, preferring to dine on tempura and teriyaki chicken. In fact, even obtaining fresh fish for the various Japanese restaurants he worked in in Vancouver was a challenge.

But Tojo turned things around by turning things inside out—literally. While working at the four-seat Jinya on West Broadway in 1974, he turned a maki roll inside out, putting the seaweed inside and the rice outside, encasing avocado and local crab to create the Tojo Maki. He later renamed it the California Roll, after the only people who would eat sushi: the LA out-of-towners who were much more familiar with sashimi and maki than Vancouverites. He's also credited with creating, in 1974, the ever-popular BC Roll, a classic inside-out roll with barbecued salmon skin, cucumber and sesame seeds, which now can be found on virtually every sushi menu in British Columbia. In 1988, Tojo opened his eponymous restaurant, which consists of a 10-seat sushi bar, six tatami rooms and lots of western-style seating.

Today, the California Roll is synonymous with sushi in North America and can be found just about everywhere, including the grocery store's deli case, but Tojo's menu to this day does not list a California Roll (though it does reference it), instead offering its "pioneer," the Tojo Roll: Dungeness crab, avocado, spinach, egg and sesame seeds.

Tojo Roll

The original California Roll was invented at Jinya, but Hidekazu Tojo still has it on his menu at his eponymous restaurant and calls it the Tojo Roll, an inside-out maki roll, with the nori on the inside, and filled with delicious crab and egg omelette.

1. Cover the rolling mat with plastic wrap to avoid sticking. Place the nori horizontally on the mat, smooth side down.

2. Delicately spread the sushi rice evenly over the nori, taking care to preserve the fluffiness of the grains. Flip over the nori so that the rice is face down on the mat.

3. Spread the mayonnaise and wasabi along the length of the roll—approximately ⅓ inch (1 cm) from the edge closest to you—and top with the crabmeat, avocado, spinach and egg strips.

4. Starting at the edge closest to you and using the mat, roll up the filling in the rice and nori. Gently press the seam to secure and create the desired cylindrical shape. With a sharp knife, slice into six pieces.

5. Garnish with sesame seeds, and enjoy with pickled ginger.

MAKES 1 ROLL

½ nori sheet, lightly toasted

⅔ cup (160 ml) cooked seasoned sushi rice (see below)

1 Tbsp (15 ml) mayonnaise

2 tsp (10 ml) prepared wasabi

⅓ cup (80 ml) Dungeness crabmeat, boiled or steamed

¼ avocado, peeled and sliced lengthwise

6 leaves fresh spinach, blanched, water squeezed out

Egg omelette (approximately ⅛ ounce/5 g), cut into thin strips

3 Tbsp (45 ml) toasted sesame seeds

Pickled ginger, for serving

SEASONED SUSHI RICE:

1. Cook the rice in the rice cooker according to the manufacturer's instructions.

2. Whisk the sugar and salt in the vinegar until dissolved.

3. When the rice is cooked, transfer it to a large bowl.

4. Pour the vinegar mixture over the rice and lightly mix with a wooden spatula while fanning the rice. Be careful not to overmix or crush the rice.

5. Use the seasoned rice while still warm. Keep the bowl covered with a clean damp kitchen towel when not in use.

Seasoned Sushi Rice

2 rice-cooker cups' worth of Japanese rice

2 Tbsp (30 ml) granulated sugar

1 tsp (5 ml) kosher salt

⅓ cup (80 ml) rice vinegar

CHAPTER ELEVEN

The 1990s

"'Chef-owned' entered
the vernacular."

eanut shells covered the floor, suggestive cartoons lined the walls and servers clad in T-shirts they decorated themselves wrote their names on the brown paper cloaking the tables. If you didn't know about Jack Astor's satirical service methodology when it first opened in St. Catharines, Ontario, in 1990, you probably wouldn't have left a good Yelp review (if that had been a thing back then), thinking those brutish bar backs weren't very friendly. But, hey, everyone loves a good theme restaurant, right? Brian Kappler of the *Montreal Gazette* spoke of Jack Astor's in a 1997 review, explaining that "a casual restaurant, in this sense, looks a little like a theme park."

The 1990s saw the decor and theme of a restaurant become more important than ever, with the experience becoming as important as the food in both casual and high-end dining.

Outside the dining room, the decade saw dramatic shifts in the ideas of regionality as a referendum was held about one province leaving and a new Arctic territory, Nunavut, was created. "Chef-owned" entered the vernacular, as did "la cuisine régionale au Québec." This period saw the meteoric rise of Californian cuisine, which focused on hyper-local, fresh and seasonal ingredients and infiltrated evolving culinary trends, kickstarting Canadian chefs to showcase the bounty of this massive country. Slow Food, sustainability and locality became important, especially in the major cities of Vancouver, Toronto and Montreal.

North 44

TORONTO, ONTARIO (1990–2018)

When Mark McEwan opened North 44 at Yonge and Eglinton in 1990, he was only 33 years old but already had more than 15 years of experience in the kitchen. He had started working as a dishwasher in his hometown of Buffalo, New York, before attending George Brown College's culinary school. After a stint as executive chef at Sutton Place Hotel, he opened North 44.

McEwan's focus on luxe ingredients and continental methods with seasonal local ingredients shifted the Toronto dining scene forever. Think foie gras with roasted pear jam, crisp rosti, leeks and a black currant infusion followed by Pacific halibut baked in parchment with baby bok choy, a curry infusion and grilled lemon.

North 44 attracted international attention, became a regular spot for high-end diners and was a favourite of the city's critics for decades. It closed in 2018, but McEwan, touted as Toronto's first celebrity chef, went on to Food Network fame and opened many more restaurants, including Bymark and Fabbrica, and even his own grocery store chain, McEwan Fine Foods.

Klondike Kate's Restaurant

DAWSON CITY, YUKON (1990–2021)

According to historical record (and urban legend), there are many Klondike Kates. Whether you believe she was Kate Carmack, the Tagish First Nation prospector; Kate Ryan, an honourable Mountie who looked after female prisoners during the Klondike gold rush; or Kate Rockwell, the dance-hall cutie, one thing is for sure: the food at Klondike Kate's Restaurant is as Yukon as it gets. The yellow gold rush–era building sits on the corner of King and Third, with old-timey signage on all its sides. Inside, log wainscotting and black-and-white photographs of prospectors and vintage dance-hall posters line the walls, and French bistro chairs beckon diners.

Josée Savard and Philippe Lamarche opened the restaurant in 1990, adding rental cabins in the late '90s. They were extremely focused on representing their region. Travellers and locals dined on a menu that was ever-changing yet always focused on home-grown ingredients—alder-smoked pulled pork sandwiches, blackened arctic char, and bison and elk blueberry sausage. They served wines produced by First Nations vintners in British Columbia and beers from Yukon Brewing in Whitehorse. The restaurant was taken over by new owners in 2019 but closed permanently in 2021.

Zellers Family Restaurant

FREDERICTON, NEW BRUNSWICK (1991–2013)

Zellers' major expansion in the 1990s meant that there were a whole lot of new restaurants in Canada. Eventually, two restaurant motifs had made their way across the country: the diner with sparkly teal banquets, chrome chairs and an interpretation of 1950s diner decor, which came of age in the 1980s, and the demurer family restaurant, with a red and yellow decor and a simplistic cafeteria-style vibe, which was the prevalent theme of Zellers restaurants in the 1990s. Whichever it was, all those restaurants tucked into a corner of the discount department store had a few things in common: they were community meeting places, and they sold all the same menu of grilled cheese, hot hamburger sandwiches, the mini Z burger, the 3-D Club (with three layers) and, of course, the $1.99 breakfast special. In Fredericton's Brookside Mall, the restaurant was not only a champion for hiring women and a daily meeting place for retirees but also a whole event for kids and their parents. A 25-cent ride on Zeddy the teddy bear made any visit complete.

River Café

CALGARY, ALBERTA (1991–Present)

Dining on an island is not something that readily comes to mind when thinking about restaurants in the Prairies. But in Calgary, where the Bow River bends near the neighbourhood of Eau Claire, Prince's Island Park has been home to the beloved River Café for three decades. Opened in 1991 by Sal Howell and her partners at the Mescalero Group, Howell (who is now the sole owner) transformed the dilapidated park's concession stand and its handful of outdoor tables for seasonal dining into one of Calgary's most prestigious fine-dining restaurants. Howell hired Chef Dwayne Ennest in 1995, when the cafe shifted to year-round dining after realizing the full potential the magical dining experience had, and a parade of talented chefs have been honoured to run the kitchen ever since.

The interior is decidedly earthy-meets-fishing lodge, fitting in with its arboreal surroundings; the chairs are made of rough tree branches, and the place is decorated with found objects and local art. The focus on local and sustainability is on another level, with devotion paid to Indigenous and heirloom products; for instance, in place of lemons, the kitchen uses local sumac. There is no pepper, olive oil or soy sauce on the premises. If it doesn't come from Canada, it's not getting on the island. The red lentil hummus is legendary, and over the years, dishes went from simple items—like angel hair pasta with smoked salmon, and poached tomatoes stuffed with mixed grains and nuts—to more complicated dishes—for instance, roasted wild boar with local feta, and pumpkin blinis with warm duck rillette, dried cranberries and watercress.

Yukon Arctic Char *with* Broccoli, Sumac, Seared Leeks *and* Avonlea–Buttermilk Sauce

Recipe from the River Café

Chef Scott MacKenzie is the newest executive chef at this Calgary dining institution, and he serves this summery dish using every part of a head of broccoli, from the tips of the dark green part—fried with sumac to make a crumb—to the dense stem—sliced thin with a mandolin.

BROCCOLI PURÉE

1. Slice the small broccoli stems and set them aside.

2. In a large heavy-bottomed pot set over medium heat, melt the butter. Add the sliced broccoli stems and cook until almost tender.

3. Add the cream and milk, and reduce until the liquid coats the broccoli.

4. Transfer the mixture to a blender along with the spinach, and purée. Add salt to taste.

5. Prepare an ice bath, and set another large bowl overtop. Pass the purée through a chinois or fine-mesh sieve into the bowl. Set aside, and reserve the ice bath.

SERVES 6

Broccoli Purée

3¾ cups (925 ml) broccoli stems

¼ cup (60 ml) unsalted butter

¾ cup + 1 Tbsp (190 ml) heavy cream

¾ cup + 1 Tbsp (190 ml) whole milk

1⅓ cups (325 ml) fresh spinach

Salt, to taste

Recipe continues…

AVONLEA-BUTTERMILK SAUCE

1. Heat the buttermilk in a small saucepan over low heat, then transfer to a blender, add roasted garlic and purée. Then slowly add the Avonlea cheddar in small chunks and blend until emulsified.

2. Set a large bowl overtop the reserved ice bath. Pass the purée through a chinois or a fine-mesh sieve into the bowl and set aside. Reserve the ice bath.

BROCCOLI SUMAC CRUMB

1. Fill a large, heavy-bottomed pot one-third of the way with canola oil and set over medium-high heat. Heat the oil to 400°F (200°C).

2. Fry the broccoli florets in the oil until crispy, then transfer to a plate lined with paper towel to drain and cool. Once cooled, toss the florets with the sumac to coat.

LEEK ROUNDS

1. Bring a pot of water to a boil.

2. Slice the leek into ½-inch (1.2 cm) pieces and put in the boiling water. Steam or blanch until tender, about 1 minute. Scoop out and transfer to a plate lined with paper towel, to drain. Reserve the boiling water for blanching the broccoli.

Avonlea-Buttermilk Sauce

2 cups (500 ml) buttermilk

2 Tbsp (30 ml) roasted garlic

1 cup (250 ml) Avonlea cheddar cheese

Salt, to taste

Broccoli Sumac Crumb

Canola oil, for frying

2 cups (500 ml) broccoli florets

1 Tbsp (15 ml) sumac

Leek Rounds

1 leek, white part only, rinsed well

ARCTIC CHAR AND BROCCOLI

1. Preheat the oven to 400°F (200°C) and line a baking sheet with parchment paper.

2. Slice the large broccoli stems thinly on a mandolin.

3. Bring the water used to blanch the leeks back to a boil. Add the broccoli stems and blanch until tender, about 30 seconds. Transfer to the ice bath.

4. Divide the arctic char filets into six portions, and place on the baking sheet.

5. Bake the filets for 5 minutes, then remove the skins, and return to the oven until they flake easily when tested with a fork. Remove from the oven and sprinkle with the broccoli crumb.

6. Heat the broccoli purée, then transfer to a serving platter.

7. Heat the Avonlea-buttermilk sauce in a small pot and fold in the broccoli stems. Once hot, place on the platter.

8. Add a splash of olive oil to a frying pan set over medium heat. Sear the cooked leeks in the oil until golden brown. Transfer to the platter.

9. Place the arctic char on top of the sauce and serve immediately.

Arctic Char and Broccoli

3 large broccoli stems

3 arctic char filets, pinbones removed

Bánh Mì Thi-Thi

CALGARY, ALBERTA (1991–Present)

Many Calgarians know this Vietnamese sub shop as "the one by the Harry Hays Building," and the federal civil servants working there do often come across the street to join this popular Chinatown sandwich shop's queue, which is always long no matter how low the temperature drops. Hoa Nguyen and his wife, Hoa Tran, opened the doors to Bánh Mì Thi-Thi on April 9, 1991, at 9 a.m.; it was the first of dozens of Vietnamese sub shops to crop up in Calgary over the past 30 years. Vietnamese subs are now one of the most popular street foods in the city, which has the second most Vietnamese restaurants in the country after Vancouver (there's even a drive-thru on the Macleod Trail called To Me).

The signature sub at Thi-Thi's is the sate beef, which comes with all the expected accoutrement—mayo, pâté, white onions, daikon and pickled carrots, cucumber, cilantro, Thai chilies and cheese—topped with fish sauce and soy sauce before being stuffed inside a crusty French baguette. Thi-Thi's Chinatown location, which Nguyen runs with his son, Binh, is takeout only, and many subbers like to walk down to the nearby river and eat with a view.

Right: Hoa Nguyen and his wife, Hoa Tran

Vanipha Lanna

TORONTO, ONTARIO (1993–2011)

Vanipha Southalack has left a trail of noodles across Toronto. When she came as a refugee from Laos in 1980, the Thai-born cook worked in Queen Street West kitchens, including at the Queen Mother Cafe and the Rivoli, frying up pad Thai and spring rolls when few others were doing it (pad Thai is still on both restaurants' menus, and Southalack supplied their spring rolls for a decade after she left). In 1989, she opened Vanipha Fine Cuisine near Kensington Market with her brother-in-law, Peter Thavone, before heading north to Eglinton, where she set up her own spot, churning out the crispy egg rolls she had become known for.

The small dining room on Eglinton served up complex Lanna (Northern Thai) and Laotian flavours: laab gai with lime-chili dressing; salad rolls with Thai basil, pickled carrots and roast duck; Thai dumplings with a bean-curd wrapper; and fresh mango salads, not to mention bowls and bowls of curries and soups. She expanded to St. Clair Avenue West in 2002, to a strip mall plaza with her daughter Noonie. Both locations closed in 2011, and since then they have been operating Vanipha Asian Gourmet, a retail and catering operation.

Toqué!

MONTREAL, QUEBEC (1993–Present)

Normand Laprise and Christine Lamarche were part of the fine-dining detachment that bid *adieu* to stuffy French methodology and presentation, and they did so in Quebec style. The pair met working at Montreal's Citrus in the early 1990s, leaving together to open Toqué! in 1993 and ushering in Quebec's era of nouvelle cuisine with a menu that was ingredient-driven above all else. Their laser focus on building strong relationships with their purveyors, including local producers, in part to offer traceability for every dish has shifted the way chefs across the

Foie Gras Terrine from Toqué! restaurant

country shop for ingredients. Even from the beginning of their 55-seat restaurant on rue Saint-Denis, cost was no object for them—they ordered whatever they wanted, whenever they wanted it, from across North America, whether it was lobster from Nova Scotia or squash from Kentucky. But the focus has always remained on local Québécois ingredients, like Cap-Saint-Ignace quail lamb from Île Verte, and foie gras terrine and cheeses from local fromageries.

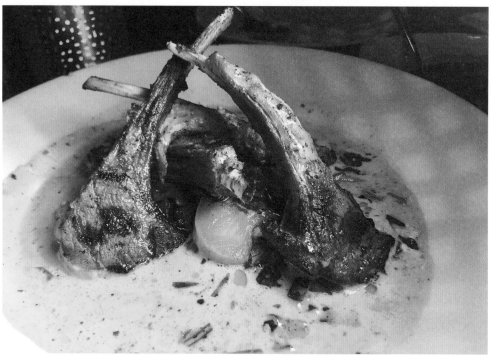

Vij's

VANCOUVER, BRITISH COLUMBIA (1994–Present)

South Granville Street got a South Asian glow-up in the 1990s. Vikram Vij was born and raised in Amritsar, India, immigrating to Canada in 1989 after studying hotel management and culinary arts in Austria. When he eventually landed in Vancouver, he went to work for Chef John Bishop (his story is on page 206), before going out on his own. In 1994, thanks to some savings and a paper bag filled with cash from his father, Vij opened his first restaurant, named Vij's after his grandfather, on West Broadway. His then-wife, Meeru Dhalwala, joined soon after, managing the predominantly-female kitchen while Vij ran front-of-house.

At first, business was slow; patrons were expecting Westernized iterations of Indian fare. But soon, their use of local ingredients and traditional Indian cooking techniques changed how Canadians, and the world, viewed Indian cuisine.

Despite having to move down the street in 1996 after the landlord complained about the restaurant's aromatics, success came. Vij's wine-marinated lamb popsicles with fenugreek cream curry have become legendary, not to mention his BC pork tenderloin smothered in cayenne curry, jackfruit coconut curry, and cauliflower pakoras, all served on locally made pottery, along with an array of cocktails infused with Indian flavours. Vij and his wife followed up with Rangoli right next door in 2004 and have gone on to open more restaurants, pump out cookbooks and appear regularly on the Food Network.

Max & Moritz Spicy Island Food House

GALIANO ISLAND, BRITISH COLUMBIA (1995–Present)

Waiting in line for a ferry is commonplace in British Columbia's Gulf Islands. Carpoolers, cyclists and pedestrians fall into rank expectantly as they island-hop as part of a daily commute or a relaxing vacation. And while onboard cafe services abound (White Spot burgers are available on several routes; their story is on page 86), it's in the ferry lineups where one can grab salmon burgers, clam chowder and even Indonesian-German fare.

Lucy Reksoatmodjo immigrated to British Columbia from Germany in 1995

Owner Lucy Reksoatmodjo with her daughter, Anna, and sister, Julie

with her then husband Christian Banski and dreamt of opening a food truck, something they had great affection for—they were popular in the couple's hometown of Berlin. After Vancouver's strict food-truck rules proved impenetrable, they went to the BC Ferries office, begging for permission to set up at a ferry terminal.

Max & Moritz Spicy Island Food House opened shop with a bright red food cart soon after, at the Sturdies Bay Ferry Terminal on Galiano Island. The pair found great success with German street food, but as the years passed, Reksoatmodjo (who is now the sole owner) wanted to serve up both German food and food from her natal country of Indonesia. Now people line up within a lineup for Max & Moritz's stir-fried nasi goreng, piping hot currywurst served on a bun with sautéed onions, and all-day breakfasts, all of which have been feeding ferry riders for decades.

Gandhi Indian Cuisine

TORONTO, ONTARIO (1995–2020)

In 2001, Canadian food writer Jacob Richler called roti Toronto's "smoked meat," and he was not wrong. The Caribbean dish is omnipresent in the city's culinary landscape, and so is its East Indian offspring, butter chicken roti.

Avtar Singh came to Canada in the 1970s, working first as a dishwasher, then landing a cooking gig at Babur restaurant on Queen Street. After he tried Caribbean roti for the first time—in Toronto in the 1980s—and fell in love with the dish, Singh was inspired to make his own version using family curry recipes to create a West Indian roti jam-packed with East Indian curries.

He opened Gandhi Indian Cuisine on Queen Street West in 1995 in an old fish-and-chips shop that had an open kitchen and only a few tables. He began serving up huge flour roti cooked on a flat griddle and filled with butter chicken, then folded into a rectangular aluminum tray, which fed two people and needed to be sliced open from the top and eaten with a knife and fork (the messiness wouldn't allow for any other way). The dish became incredibly popular, and soon Singh expanded the menu to include other favourites—channa, tikka masala, saag paneer—all cubed inside that huge folded roti.

And so, a Toronto iconic dish was born and replicated across the Greater Toronto Area; there are few spots in the city that aren't somehow connected to Gandhi Indian Cuisine. When Singh announced his retirement in 2020 during the COVID-19 pandemic, the outcry on social media could be heard across the city, and many lined up for one last taste of the trend-making roti.

Liliget Feast House

VANCOUVER, BRITISH COLUMBIA (1995–2007)

Pan flute music played as diners were led along a wooden path lined with stones that divided the dining room tables made of cedar planks. The longhouse, designed by architect Arthur Erickson, was the home of Liliget Feast House, the name being a very literal translation considering that "liliget" means "the place the people come to feast" in the Gitk'san language. Opened at the corner of Denman and Davie Streets in 1995, it was the first First Nations restaurant in North America. Owners Dolly Watts, a residential school survivor, and her daughter Annie Watts, presented patrons with baskets of bannock with a smoked-salmon cream cheese spread, smoked oolichan with lemon, and alder-grilled venison chops with savoury rhubarb sauce.

The Pointe Restaurant at the Wickaninnish Inn

TOFINO, BRITISH COLUMBIA (1996–Present)

Tofino, the coastal escape as we know it today, wasn't accessible by road until the 1950s. But it soon garnered a reputation for respite thanks to its breathtaking beaches. Hoards of conscientious objectors and hippies flocked there in the 1960s. It has remained relaxed, and even the most acclaimed restaurant in Tofino requires only casual attire.

In 1996, father and son team George and Charles McDiarmid opened The Pointe at the Wickaninnish Inn on a parcel of land on the north end of Chesterman Beach that they had purchased in the 1970s. The restaurant became a beacon for progressive and sustainable culinary practices, and an incubator for up-and-coming chefs. The inn basically made Tofino what it is today, putting it on the map for tourists, surfers and culinary travellers. The round dining room's peaked ceiling is mirrored in the glinting copper of the 360-degree roaring fireplace. A perfect place for storm-watching over dinner.

Top: Oyster with Winter Radishes and Preserved Wild Huckleberry from The Pointe

Bottom Left: Interior of Liliget Feast House

Bottom Right: Liliget Feast House server James Joseph

Chez Christophe

GROSSES COQUES, NOVA SCOTIA (1997–2012)

Acadian food isn't typically thought of as restaurant food but rather as a homey, traditional set of dishes. But dining at Chez Christophe felt just like coming home. Housed in the 1857 homestead of Chef Paul Comeau, the restaurant took up three rooms of the historic property, including the old kitchen where the woodstove still stood. It opened its doors in 1997 on the French Shore of Nova Scotia, where Acadians have been cooking for hundreds of years, once they'd trickled back to the province following the Grand Dérangement of the mid-1750s.

Traditional Acadian dishes that aren't easily found in restaurants—think rappie pie or chicken fricot with dumplings— were served alongside seafood chowder, pan-fried scallops and creamed lobster on toast with potatoes, typically as feet stomping to live music bent the wooden floorboards.

The restaurant closed in 2012 when Comeau passed away, but these days, Nadine and Scott Robicheau operate La Cuisine Robicheau at the same location. Nadine spent seven years working at Chez Christophe and still serves rappie pie, poutines râpée and generous bowls of chowder.

Kintaro Ramen

VANCOUVER, BRITISH COLUMBIA (1999–Present)

Ramen Row occupies the western end of Robson Street in downtown Vancouver, with almost a dozen noodle shops interspersed with Korean BBQ, Chinese takeouts and mom-and-pop shops. But when Daiji Matsubara opened his spot, Kintaro, in 1999, seven years after arriving from Tokyo, ramen was an almost unknown dish in the city.

Kintaro was one of the first ramen restaurants in Vancouver and a pioneer of the soupy, noodly dish. There isn't much to Kintaro: the black awning outside leads into a small spot with a few tables and stools that sidle up to a bar overlooking the open kitchen filled with steaming vats of broth and boiling pots of water for noodles. But the flavours have been unmatched for more than 20 years. The tonkatsu-based pork bone broth simmers for almost 24 hours so that it's dense and creamy. There's only ramen on the menu as mains, along with a few sides, such as gyoza.

CHAPTER TWELVE

The 2000s

"Nose to table, farm to table–the 2000s in Canada were all about bringing it to the table."

On Tuesday evenings in the mid-2000s, *Made to Order* aired just before the big guns from the US-based Food Network, the Barefoot Contessa and Emeril, lit up televisions across Canada. The restaurant reality show starred the Rubino Brothers, with Michael as chef and Guy at front-of-house. The brothers were the headliner 2000s Toronto restaurateurs behind the famed Zoom, Rain and Luce, and on *Made to Order*, diners from across the country got an inside look at how a restaurant actually worked. The show skyrocketed in popularity, airing in 150 countries during its three-year run.

Food Network Canada launched at the beginning of the 2000s and catapulted restaurant chefs to stardom. With the proliferation of food media flourishing beyond the typical newspaper restaurant critics, chef-run restaurants meant that a new wave of sustainable, ingredient-focused restaurants were being Yelped about across the country. Nose to table, farm to table—the 2000s in Canada were all about bringing it to the table. Hyper-local became the top priority for high-end dining and changed the way we use the term, with diners becoming increasingly concerned with where their food came from and how it was processed. Restaurants, from casual chains to coffee shops, started to identify healthy choice options on their menus. The 2000s also saw a rise in popularity in gourmet food trucks in Canada. These weren't just your usual chip trucks pumping out cheap and cheerful french fries, think fried chicken and waffles, bowls of fresh pasta and beef tongue bao buns.

Fid

HALIFAX, NOVA SCOTIA (2000–2013)

As the Slow Food and farm-to-table movements made their way across the country, Fid, in Halifax, was at the forefront of both. Chef Dennis Johnston had apprenticed in London, learning classic French and Japanese techniques, then worked in Switzerland, France and England before ending up in Montreal, where he met his wife Monica Bauché, who had come to Montreal from France. They worked in high-end restaurants in Montreal before returning to Halifax to open Fid.

Fid opened in 2000 and, with the help of other restaurants, like Chives Canadian Bistro and Maple Bistro, they reshaped the production of agriculture in Nova Scotia. These restaurants were focused on quality local ingredients, and because of the close-knit community and small size of the province, they could successfully ask producers to grow specific ingredients. This had a notable impact on the local ingredients available. For instance, for a specific dish, Johnston might seek out caul fat from the abattoir, which then started selling it retail, or perhaps a certain kind of squash would show up at the markets after he had requested it be grown.

Fid was also one of the first restaurants to put the producers' names on the menus, as is done in major city centres. And the best part? Because the producers were less than one hundred kilometres away, you could eat a carrot dish at Fid on Friday night and then go grab a bunch from the farmers' market on Saturday morning. Or you could enjoy an amuse-bouche of sea urchin caught the same day just 30 minutes away, grilled local goat paneer with hazelnuts and greens, and seared scallops with smoked tomatillo squash ice cream.

The name changed from Fid to Fid Resto in 2009, relaxing both the menu prices and the mood (no more white linens), and bringing fishcakes, gnocchi and the beloved Fid Burger to the menu. Their "back door pad Thai" became famous among Haligonians. When the couple's lease was up in 2013, they moved into catering, continuing to build on their more than a decade of influence in the province.

HK B.B.Q. Master

RICHMOND, BRITISH COLUMBIA (2001–Present)

Long fluorescent bulbs light up the entrance of HK B.B.Q. Master, on the underground parking floor of the Superstore complex in Richmond, its front window display glowing red like a beacon for barbecue, with sticky red sauce dripping off the hanging barbecued duck, chicken and spareribs. HK B.B.Q. Master owner Eric Leung was born in Hong Kong and got his start early in restaurants at 14 years old, proceeding to work at barbecue restaurants for almost 20 years before arriving in Canada in 1992. He continued to hone his craft, opening HK B.B.Q. Master in 2001. Brother Robbin Leung takes care of the administration side, while son Anson stepped up to learn the craft (and man the Instagram account) and is now the master.

In the beginning, the customer base consisted mostly of other Hong Kong migrants who had come to Richmond after the 1997 exchange of power in Hong Kong, but slowly and surely, the restaurant has become one of the most popular spots for anyone wanting to grab some crispy roasted pork, though the patronage still skews toward Cantonese speakers. Just ask David Chang, who visited in 2019 on his Netflix series *Ugly Delicious* with Vancouver-born actor Seth Rogan.

Au Pied de Cochon

MONTREAL, QUEBEC (2001–Present)

Au Pied de Cochon often gets lumped into the fine-dining category on the best-of Montreal lists, but it is most decidedly not in that category, or at least it wasn't when it first opened. Perhaps it helped redefine the term. Chef-owner Martin Picard worked in fine-dining restaurant kitchens for years before chucking out the fancy coat for a dirty apron. "The Wild Chef" opened Au Pied de Cochon in 2001, aiming to create a brasserie that focused on high-quality ingredients. It quickly became a quintessential Montreal restaurant. Convivial and loud, it serves up a richness found on no other tasting menus in the city.

In the restaurant, it feels as if there is wood everywhere: wood floors give way to the long-burnished wood bar cordoning off the open kitchen, which is mirrored by the whole length of the dining room. When Picard first opened the place, there was seemingly foie gras on everything. The most outrageously beloved dish? Foie gras poutine. This dish is said to be responsible for the trend of putting just about anything on poutine, from butter chicken to po'boys. Being catapulted into fame by the adoring words of Anthony Bourdain didn't hurt either.

Grassmere Family Restaurant

WEST ST. PAUL, MANITOBA (2004–Present)

It's no wonder Filipino chicken chain Jollibee chose Winnipeg for its first Canadian location. The Prairie city has one of the highest populations of Filipinos in North America and it's still rising. In the 1980s, newly immigrated Filipinos started working in other people's kitchens, and it wasn't until the early 2000s that Filipino restaurants entered the Canadian dining vernacular. It's now become a much-loved cuisine across the Prairies and the entire country.

Macario and Rosalina Cabungcal emigrated from the Philippines in the 1980s, taking over the Grassmere Family Restaurant in West St. Paul in 2004 when their sons Charlie and Carlo were still in high school. For a decade they continued the eatery's traditional menu of Canadian-style breakfasts and cheeseburgers, but in 2014 they started serving Filipino dishes like tapsilog and sinigang at the request of their loyal patrons.

Once the boys entered the business, they started experimenting with new dishes— tall stacks of bright purple ube pancakes (which became Instagram famous), and tocino fries with sweet pork, pico de gallo and garlic sour cream, topped with an egg—that have made Grassmere a brunch destination.

D Hot Shoppe

BURLINGTON, ONTARIO (2005–Present)

Caribbean roti is abundant in the Greater Toronto Area, and what a long way it has travelled: first from India to the Caribbean in the 19th century, when enslaved people brought the recipe with them, using the roti as a flatbread to spoon up their curries, then from the Caribbean, where until the mid-20th century it got wrapped up in tinfoil as a wrapping for street food, to Canada, where it began to be eaten with a knife and fork (by some people).

At D Hot Shoppe, the flavours of Trinidad and Tobago are hot—six-pepper-scale hot. Gabriel Lou-Hing came to Canada in 1993, his wife Simone joined him in 2004, and within a year they opened up their own restaurant. Simone, who had trained in real estate, was working at a Tim Hortons and Gabriel at his aunt's roti shop when they decided to move to Burlington and open their own roti shop. Gabriel had spent years cheffing in hotels in Antigua and Trinidad, but really it was his nanny, mother and grandmother who taught him everything he knows.

Rotis filled with curried potatoes, goat, chicken or cuttlefish fly out the door of this strip mall shop, which has just a few tables and a Pepsi machine filled with Ting to the right of the cash. At first, most of their Canadian patrons ate their roti with a fork and knife, which Gabriel and Simone found odd, but soon all the patrons were asking for forks, and an extra spoonful of sauce poured overtop.

Japadog

VANCOUVER, BRITISH COLUMBIA (2005–Present)

Talk about born-again street food. Japadog reincarnated an old favourite into a delicious mashup of cuisines and culture that is now so representative of Vancouver's dining scene. The first time Noriki Tamura and his wife, Misa, travelled abroad was when they immigrated to Canada from Japan in 2005, with dreams of opening a food cart. Initially, Tamura had dreamed up a variety of Japanese-style menu items to sell from the food cart, but Vancouver's strict street-food bylaws prevented him from selling anything but hot dogs. So instead of selling the typical American-style hot dogs with mustard and ketchup, Tamura integrated his Japanese heritage right into the bun—or between the buns, I should say. And thus the Japadog was born, on the corner of Burrard and Smithe Streets, near the Sutton Place Hotel, where it still stands today.

Now there are more than 10 Japadogs to choose from, like the fan favourite Terimayo, with teriyaki sauce, mayonnaise and chiffonaded seaweed overflowing from the bun, or the Okonomi—Kurobuta sausage topped with bonito flakes. Within weeks of opening, Japadog had developed a following of loyal lunchers willing to wait in line for their Yakiniku Rice and Ebi Tempura hot dogs. The Tamuras had introduced Japanese flavours to a whole new audience. With the rise in popularity of fancy food trucks chauffeuring high-end cuisine at rallies across Canada, the Tamuras saw further success, expanding Japadog. By 2011, they had five carts across the city, a trailer and a food truck, plus a brick-and-mortar restaurant on Robson Street. In 2014, Japadog went international with two stands in Los Angeles.

The Star Cafe

MAPLE CREEK, SASKATCHEWAN (2007–2018)

Prairie boomtowns along the railroad have many old buildings that have lived many lives, and most don't get revitalized like they do in Maple Creek. Tina Cresswell and her husband, Dave Turner, opened the Star Cafe in 2007 after spending more than $100,000 restoring the building. It was a reincarnation and restoration of an 1898 structure that had housed dozens of restaurants since its origins as a CPR offshoot hotel, including a Chinese-Canadian eatery that bore the same name. With the renovation, the restaurant was transformed from

a convenience eatery to a welcoming casual fine-dining spot. Its stone walls, stained glass and communal vibe were a tribute to the town's yesteryear and helped revitalize Maple Creek by putting it on the culinary-destination map of Saskatchewan.

The Star's international menu reflected the parade of chefs who headed up the kitchen over the years, with dishes like Guyanese jerk chicken, Thai lettuce wraps and the signature shrimp and chicken penne—a reflection of the couple's devotion to teaching and supporting immigrant cooks. They still run a local coffee shop, the Daily Grind, in another historic building they restored in 2005.

Bacalao

ST. JOHN'S, NEWFOUNDLAND AND LABRADOR
(2007–2018)

The influence of the Portuguese on Newfoundland and Labrador cuisine isn't evident despite their close relationship the province thanks to shared fishing grounds and the love of one particular fish: cod. The mutual love affair for bacalao was Andrea Maunder's inspiration when she opened her restaurant of the same name in 2007. Maunder's reinvigoration of traditional Newfoundland dishes with a heavy focus on local producers was something not seen in St. John's before.

Bacalao, with its "nouvelle Newfoundland cuisine," was housed in a historic home on Lemarchant Road, which still is home to a stretch of fish-merchant mansions. The parlour and dining room of this former home was once filled with patrons dunking egg rolls stuffed with fresh Newfoundland crab into a dipping sauce made from bakeapples (the rest of Canada knows them as cloudberries); devouring a traditional Jiggs dinner, albeit wrapped in cabbage and then steamed, plus a shot of the pot liquor and mustard pickles; forking grilled Labrador caribou and blueberry salad; or dismantling fresh lobster tails coated with spruce cream sauce.

The Black Hoof

TORONTO, ONTARIO (2008–2018)

There are restaurants, and then there are places like the Black Hoof. As one of the most famous restaurants in Toronto's history, it ushered in changes to how Toronto dined out: no tablecloths, no reservations, all ambience and meat. Along with Chef Grant van Gameren (who went on to open his own series of restaurants), a young Jen Agg opened the Black Hoof on a part of Dundas West that wasn't anywhere on the trendy scale. Agg's menus celebrated off-cuts and charcuterie. The kitchen brought in two and a half gallons of pig's blood a week for their blood custard with rosemary and pickled pears. Other dishes included beef heart tartare, foie gras with Nutella, and roasted bone marrow luge, which Anthony Bourdain claimed was an essential Toronto dining experience after demolishing the marrow and getting bourbon poured down his throat by Agg herself. Speaking of cocktails, they were so good at the Hoof that Agg opened the simply named Cocktail Bar across the street in 2011, plus several more restaurants, each with a major focus on lighting, decor and music. Good vibes all around.

Tacofino

TOFINO, BRITISH COLUMBIA (2009–Present)

The little orange truck that could . . . start a taco empire. When Kaeli Robinsong and Jason Sussman started up the engine to their taco truck parked behind Live to Surf surfing school at Chesterman Beach, it was meant to feed hungry surfers after catching waves off Tofino's iconic beaches. Instead, they created a food-truck phenomenon. The vibe of the truck was very Baja-Cali style; the ingredients, wedged between soft tortillas, West Coast–inspired. The fish tacos, including the Tuna-ta Taco—a taco with seared albacore, wasabi mayo, wakame and pickled ginger—are staples on the menu, as is tortilla soup. Other tacos, like the crispy karaage chicken and guac, or the pickled cauliflower with achiote onion, lime crema and salsa verde, change on the regular. A second truck came in 2011, then they opened their first brick-and-mortar restaurant in Vancouver on East Hastings in 2012 and, like a wave, opened more than a dozen restaurants and trucks in Tofino, Victoria and Vancouver.

CHAPTER THIRTEEN

The 2010s

"Exit white tablecloths,
enter stunt food."

Exit white tablecloths, enter stunt food. Instagram photos of milkshakes piled high with whipped cream, candy and full-sized doughnuts held in front of a brick wall by a floating hand; Caesars overflowing with bacon, fried chicken and breakfast sandwiches as garnishes at The Beltline in Calgary; and who could forget the Ziggy Stardust Disco Egg at La Banane in Toronto, where you cracked open a huge chocolate egg graffitied with chocolate and filled with treats?

The 2010s saw the rise of Instagram, social media and the peak of bloggers, yelpers and anyone with a smartphone who had an opinion about where they ate (and the pictures to prove it). Social media made the way a dish photographed as important as what it tasted like; ditto for what your restaurant looked like.

Farm to table went into hyperdrive with diners' appreciation for local and regional cuisine, and veganism went mainstream with high-end plant-based restaurants like PLANTA in Toronto and the "Impossible" burger becoming a staple on menus across the country. Indigenous restaurants started to grow in number as Indigenous chefs showcased their traditional recipes and ingredients on luxe tasting menus such as that at the Keriwa Cafe, as well as via food trucks and family eateries.

Reykjavik Cafe

GIMLI, MANITOBA (2010–2015)

Vinarterta, one of the most beloved sweets synonymous with Iceland, isn't actually very popular there. But head to Manitoba and it's all the rage. From the 1870s to the 1910s, more than a quarter of Iceland's population left the frigid island amid an economic downturn and a volcanic eruption. A few hundred of them ended up settling in New Iceland, which is known as Gimli, Manitoba, today, where there are now tens of thousands of Icelandic descendants. While vinarterta, with its plethora of labour-intensive layers, went out of vogue in Iceland centuries ago, in Gimli it's still an honoured recipe, made often for special occasions (particularly Christmas), and when Birgir Robertsson opened Reykjavik Cafe in 2010, it took off like gangbusters. Robertsson emigrated from Iceland in 2009 after selling his bar just two months before the economic collapse of 2008 and took advantage of the Canadian Government's encouragement for Icelanders to move to Gimli. He opened Viking Bakery in Toronto in 2015. Now in Gimli, Sugar Me Cookie Boutique, owned by Michelle Wierda, is the place to grab a vinarterta.

Grumman '78

MONTREAL, QUEBEC (2010–2020)

Meals on wheels were banned in Montreal for more than half a century. In 1947, the city outlawed food carts and trucks to protect public health and promote sanitation, and while one of most gastronomic cities in the country is ahead of the curve when it comes to most trends, it missed the boat on this one. Enter Grumman '78.

After a trip to Mexico where they fell in love with roadside taco stands, Marc-André Leclerc and Hilary McGown teamed up with Gaëlle Cerf to create the bright green taco truck they bought on Kijiji for $3,500. It got its engines started in 2010 and, by summer, the team was serving up tacos anywhere they were allowed, which weren't many places—no public squares or side streets. They quickly found success with private functions and festivals like the POP Montreal music festival, where they served tacos from 11 p.m. to 3 a.m. Soon other trucks joined the food fleet.

As culinarians and community activists, the crew at Grumman '78 always believed that anything prohibiting creativity and inclusion should be challenged, so they were loud lobbyists against the archaic food-truck prohibitions. And the truck stopped there. The City recanted the regulation in 2013, making the culinary landscape in Montreal a bit more mobile. Eventually, the Grumman '78 truck parked next to their rue Saint-Henri bricks-and-mortar, serving tacos piled high with homemade halibut gravlax, rhubarb relish and poblano cream, or local lamb with mango chutney and apple—accompanied by bags of horchata with a straw sticking out the top. They closed in 2020, saying the pandemic crippled their business.

Exterior of restaurant with owner Hilary McGowan and chef Sebastien Harrison Cloutier

Salmon n' Bannock

VANCOUVER, BRITISH COLUMBIA (2010–Present)

As a Sixties Scoop survivor, Inez Cook, born a member of the Nuxalk Nation, learned to love cooking while making perogies with the Mennonite-descended family she grew up with, but she yearned for her ancestral traditions. She worked in the service industry as a teenager, and spent countless hours researching Indigenous ingredients and cooking techniques. Cook opened Salmon n' Bannock in February 2010 with Remi Caudron, taking over sole ownership in 2019 and continuing her emphasis on local First Nations producers and the hiring of an all-Indigenous staff.

Found at 1128 West Broadway on the traditional territory of the Musqueam, Tsleil-Waututh, and Squamish Nations, Salmon n' Bannock's red-and-black decor showcases Indigenous art (all the art on the walls is for sale), and one's eye can't help but go to the painted canoe that hangs from the ceiling.

Diners start with charcuterie boards loaded with boar salami, dried bison and cedar jelly, with a side of bannock, followed by salmon burgers with Ojibwe wild rice or elk-shoulder osso bucco paired with Okanagan wines from Nk'Mip Cellars, the first Indigenous-owned winery in North America.

Raymonds

ST. JOHN'S, NEWFOUNDLAND AND LABRADOR
(2010–2020)

The cod sounds at Raymonds. No, it's not the sound a cod makes. (Do they make a sound?) It's the air bladder of a cod, deep-fried until its texture resembles that of chicharron. With dishes like this, Raymonds has achieved mythic status in Newfoundland and Labrador, celebrated for shifting the culinary perspective of both locals and CFAs (come-from-aways). The new-Nordic-meets-Newfoundland tasting menus have garnered international acclaim for their elevation of local and foraged ingredients, a staunch departure from the expected dishes coming out of the province, like deep-fried fish and chips.

Owners and locally grown themselves, Chef Jeremy Charles and sommelier Jeremy Bonia ("the Jeremys," as they are known) have worked together a long time, first at Atlantica, where they made it the place to dine in the city.

They renovated the Commercial Cable Company Building, a two-storey built in Classical Revival style in 1915, on the east end of Water Street, and opened their impeccably designed dining room in 2010 to much fanfare after two years of renovations.

The tall windows of the dining room shed evening light reflecting off St. John's harbour as the first courses of the evening make their way up the dumbwaiter from the expansive kitchen downstairs. Beef tartare sheltered by a phalanx of nasturtiums, turbot with uni and carrot, cod sounds topped with caviar, and pasta showered in chanterelles are just some of the dishes of the seasonally changing tasting menu. The cod sounds deflated with a whisper as the restaurant served their tenth, and final, New Year's Eve meal on December 31, 2020.

Harvest Eatery

SHAUNAVON, SASKATCHEWAN (2013–Present)

Harvest Eatery brought the table to the farm, and the diners followed. Chef Garrett "Rusty" Thienes moved back to his hometown of Shaunavon with his wife, Kristy, in 2013 to open Harvest Eatery and created a culinary destination. Many high-end restaurants are found in urban centres, but the couple wanted to centre the food they were serving in the community where it came from. The warmth Chef Rusty felt at his parents' dinner parties growing up has been transposed to his restaurant's dining room, where local art lines the walls, sheltered by an ornate tin ceiling. Servers make their way across the scuffed wooden floors from the open kitchen, which they affectionately call the "theatre," to serve the 45 seats. The menu is international-meets-Saskatchewan, with dishes like Red Fife steam buns made with local pork belly, Speckle Park striploin, wild boar ragu and their own take on a Niçoise salad featuring local steelhead trout decorated with edible flowers Kristy grows in the garden boxes out front.

Mallard Cottage

ST. JOHN'S, NEWFOUNDLAND AND LABRADOR
(2013–Present)

Since the 1600s, Quidi Vidi has been a home base for fishing: first for the migratory fisherfolk of England, then evolving into a small fishing village outside St. John's. Now it's a trendy neighbourhood enclave from which a few catching boats still depart, and is home to a brewery, craft shop and Mallard Cottage. Chef Todd Perrin, who grew up in St. John's and worked in kitchens from Stratford to Switzerland before opening up a few notable restaurants at home, launched Mallard Cottage with Kim Doyle, and sommelier Stephen Lee, in 2013 after spending a year renovating one of the oldest homes in "the gut" of Quidi Vidi.

The cottage, built by the Mallard family in the early 1800s, served as a private residence until 1985, when it was converted into an antique shop. Mallard Cottage put Newfoundland and Labrador cuisine, typically seen as undeveloped, uncultured and clunky, onto the Canadian culinary stage. Perrin is a supporter of the seal hunt and the use of traditional ingredients, which he uses in innovative ways—halibut with sea urchin butter sauce, cornmeal crusted fried cod cheeks with house-made aioli, mooseheart tartare with capers and potato chips, for instance. Then there's the famous Sunday brunch, along with the all-you-can-eat cake table, the offering of which diners enjoy to the sounds of local trad musicians fiddling in the corner.

Bite House

BADDECK, NOVA SCOTIA (2014–2020)

Hermitted away in the forest of Cape Breton was a farmhouse offering delicious plates of food: the Bite House. What was once the name of Bryan Picard's popular recipe blog became the name of his restaurant when the chef-owner, who grew up in French-speaking Saint-Hilaire, near Edmundston, New Brunswick, moved to Baddeck after falling in love with the century-old home in 2014. He was inspired to open a restaurant in it (cooking on a personal stove, with a regular old dishwasher). The two small dining rooms of the restaurant, which never felt quite like a restaurant in the best kind of way, were decorated with muted yellows, blues and greys—as quiet as the historic home's surroundings.

Once a year, Picard opened reservations, and they would be filled within the hour. There were only 16 seats in the restaurant, where Picard would serve nine simple courses devoted to Cape Breton's ingredients. Picard's experience cooking in restaurants from Nova Scotia to Copenhagen was showcased on the handmade ceramic plates. Halibut cheeks with mint, halved cherry tomatoes scattered seemingly haphazardly on the plate and interspersed with piped smoked cream, buckwheat and oregano, preceded braised pork with grilled red cabbage. To finish, there was ginger ice cream and pine syrup, cradled by wild blueberries and dried pumpkin.

In 2020, Picard hit the pause button on his reservation system due to COVID, making the call to offer takeout and catering services.

Acadia Wheat Honey Cake *with* Gooseberry Sorbet, Bay *and* Birch Syrup, *and* Hazelnuts

Recipe from Bite House

Chef Brian Picard's desserts are as layered as the intricacies of his meals. Cake and ice cream get a big upgrade with small producers and local ingredients at top of mind, and while this dessert requires some extra steps (and an ice cream machine), it's worth the effort.

GOOSEBERRY SORBET

1. Put the gooseberries, water and sugar in a medium saucepan set over medium heat, and bring to a simmer. Reduce the heat to low and cook for 15 minutes, or until the gooseberries are soft.

2. Leave the berries to cool for 10 minutes, then transfer to a blender and blend on high for a few minutes, until smooth.

3. Transfer the sorbet base to the fridge until completely cooled.

4. Make the sorbet in an ice cream maker following the manufacturer's directions.

ACADIAN WHEAT HONEY CAKE

1. Preheat the oven to 325°F (160°C) and line a 9-inch (23 cm) square baking pan with parchment paper.

2. In a bowl, mix together the flours, oats, baking soda and salt.

SERVES 8

Gooseberry Sorbet

2 cups (500 ml) gooseberries

1⅓ cups (330 ml) water

¾ cup (185 ml) cane sugar

Acadian Wheat Honey Cake

1 cup (250 ml) Acadian wheat flour

1 cup (250 ml) all-purpose flour

1 cup (250 ml) steel-cut oats

1 tsp (5 ml) baking soda

Pinch of sea salt

1 cup (250 ml) honey

¾ cup (185 ml) sunflower oil

⅔ cup (160 ml) buttermilk

2 eggs

1 tsp (5 ml) vanilla extract

3. In another bowl, whisk together the honey, oil, buttermilk, eggs and vanilla until smooth.

4. Fold the flour mixture into the honey mixture using a wooden spoon, then stir until combined.

5. Pour the batter into the prepared pan, and bake for 40 minutes or until golden brown and a cake tester inserted into the centre comes out clean. Transfer the cake to a wire rack to cool.

BAY AND BIRCH SYRUP

1. Heat the birch syrup, sugar, water, sherry and bay leaves in a small saucepan over medium heat. Once simmering, let cook for 2 minutes.

2. Remove from the heat and leave to infuse for 10 minutes, then transfer to a glass container to cool completely.

TO SERVE

1. Lay a piece of oat cake in eight individual bowls and spoon some sorbet beside it.

2. Drizzle each serving with 1 Tbsp of birch syrup. Garnish with a spoonful of toasted hazelnuts and a calendula, and serve immediately.

Bay and Birch Syrup

¼ cup (60 ml) birch syrup

¼ cup (60 ml) cane sugar

¼ cup (60 ml) water

1 Tbsp (15 ml) sherry

2 bay leaves

To Serve

½ cup (125 ml) hazelnuts, toasted and crushed

8 dried calendulas

Les Brumes du Coude

MONCTON, NEW BRUNSWICK (2014–Present)

When the Acadians settled along Moncton's Petitcodiac River in the 1730s, they nicknamed the region Le Coude, deriving from the Mi'kmaq term "pet-koat-kwee-ak," which means "the river that bends around back." Les Brumes du

Coude's haze of cuisines settles comfortably over the restaurant, housed on the first floor of the Acadian cultural centre in Moncton. The main dining room was once a school, and the decor betrays that past: high ceilings, exposed brick, scuffed wood floors. The narrow L-shaped bar that divides the cooking from the eating is lined with chairs reminiscent of those paired with old school desks. Chef Michel Savoie spent his childhood in Tabusintac, in the Acadian region of New Brunswick, before spending years working in kitchens in France and Montreal. He focused on tradition and heritage when it came to opening the restaurant in 2014—think French bistro angled to showcase local and seasonal ingredients, with traditional Acadian cuisine like North Shore crab with celeriac rémoulade, Bay of Fundy scallop ceviche and, of course, beef tartare.

Hand-Cut Beef Tartare

Recipe from Les Brumes du Coude

Inspired by the iconic L'Express in Montreal (their story is on page 200), Chef Michel Savoie's tartare is a staple on the menu at Les Brumes du Coude. This recipe is meant to be explored by everyone in their own way, adding at their leisure a little more capers or more parsley, less garlic or less heat. It's up to you—this is just a platform to get things started.

1. Place the shallots, garlic, capers, vinegar, paprika, salt and cayenne pepper in a blender. Blend well, until the mixture becomes a bit pasty.

2. With the motor running, slowly add the olive oil in a steady stream, blending until emulsified.

3. Gradually add 2 to 3 cups of the parsley, blending on low speed to form a paste. If necessary, add more olive oil to loosen the paste; it should be barely runny. If it doesn't drip off a spoon, you've achieved the right consistency.

4. The most important step in making this recipe is to taste test. The paste should be fairly tangy in sourness, salty at the edge of being too much and hot enough for your preference.

5. Refrigerate the paste for 1 day, if possible, or for at least a few hours so that it's able to hold the coolness of the beef.

6. Combine 1 tsp (5 ml) of the paste with the beef, adding more paste depending on your mood. Stir the paste into the meat about 20 times with a spoon to emulsify. Add Tabasco for extra heat, if you like, gently place the egg yolk on top and voilà.

7. Serve with a slice of crusty bread.

SERVES 2

1 Tbsp (15 ml) chopped shallots

5 to 6 cloves garlic

½ cup (125 ml) capers

3 Tbsp (45 ml) sherry vinegar

2 Tbsp (30 ml) smoked paprika

1 tsp (5 ml) kosher salt, plus more to taste

½ tsp (2 ml) cayenne pepper

1 cup (250 ml) olive oil, plus more as needed

3 to 4 cups (750 ml to 1 L) chopped flat-leaf parsley

5½ ounces (150 g) raw beef tenderloin, finely diced

Tabasco, to finish (optional)

1 raw egg yolk, for garnish

Crusty bread, for serving

Wayfarer Oyster House

WHITEHORSE, YUKON (2014–Present)

On the outside, the Wayfarer Oyster House looks like any sheet-metal shop in Whitehorse: boxy and non-descript. But inside, the Wayfarer Oyster House is anything but typical Whitehorse. The long bar is backed with blue mosaic tiles, and an oyster-shell chandelier hangs from the soaring ceiling—the DIY decor landed them on *EnRoute* magazine's Best New Restaurant list in 2019 for best design. (In 2022, Wayfarer announced it would be moving inside Polarity Brewing, but don't worry, they brought the chandelier with them.)

Chef Brian Ng, along with co-owners Eddie Rideout and Andrew Seymour, started catering and holding shucking pop-ups in 2014, eventually opening the restaurant in 2018. The menu matches the eclectic decor. Ng grew up with restaurant-owning parents and his menu has some Chinese and French flair, with a focus on local ingredients, particularly seafood. Fresh oysters, flown in fresh several times a week (not an easy feat in the North), are always on offer, and cavatelli and soba sit side by side on the menu. Rotating dishes include torchon foie gras with Thai basil and strawberry, seared scallops with enoki mushrooms, and roasted sablefish in green pea curry.

Chef and owner Michael Smith

FireWorks Feast at the Inn at Bay Fortune

SOURIS, PRINCE EDWARD ISLAND (2015–Present)

Even chefs can come home again. American-born chef Michael Smith had been working as the chef of the Inn at Bay Fortune in Souris, Prince Edward Island, since 1992, when he pitched his first TV show, *The Inn Chef*, in 1998. Fast-forward to 2015, when, several successful TV shows and dozens of cookbooks later, Smith, along with his wife, Chastity, came back to the Island, bought the 17-room inn outright and started the FireWorks Feast, which has become a food lovers' bucket-list phenomenon.

FireWorks Feast is more than an alfresco banquet; it's a journey dedicated to the bounty of Prince Edward Island, showcasing the talents of farmer Kevin Petrie. Diners start, cocktail in hand, with a tour through the gardens and greenhouses, then enjoy oysters and other apps in the garden before heading to the long communal dinner table. There they'll find the wrought-iron bread tree filled with house-made breads, pâtés and preserves, and a seafood-chowder kettle, and dine on smoked chicken legs with butter confit potatoes and liquid chicken. The evening finishes with a bonfire and s'mores.

Feast Cafe Bistro

WINNIPEG, MANITOBA (2015–Present)

Bannock's history in Canada is complicated. Some Indigenous people view the fry bread as a colonialist survival food and as non-traditional, since the wheat flour it's made with was introduced by European settlers (the Scots created the dish). Others celebrate the food as a foundational component of their culinary history.

Dishes like Indian tacos—bannock topped with Tex-Mex ingredients—are something that Peguis First Nation chef Christa Bruneau-Guenther wanted to focus on when she opened her restaurant, Feast Cafe Bistro, in 2015. Having sharpened her culinary chops as the owner of a holistic Indigenous daycare, where she was legally obligated to follow Canada's Food Guide, Bruneau-Guenther was used to getting creative with the amalgamation of traditional methods and modern ingredients. Local bison and cheddar dominate the menu of this Winnipeg Indigenous restaurant, one of the first in the province, which showcases contemporary dishes like pizza, poutine and tacos made with First Nations ingredients. You'll find wild rice and Saskatoon berries in the house salad, bannock pizzas with alder-smoked bacon and Manitoba grass-fed bison sausage, and Manitoba pickerel sliders with dill-chive aioli. Bruneau-Guenther calls her Indian tacos—consisting of traditional bannock piled high with bison chili, shredded lettuce, local Bothwell cheddar, bean and corn salsa, and maple chipotle lime sour cream—"Tipi Tacos."

Indigenous Traditional Bison Tacos

Recipe from
Feast Cafe Bistro

Bannock is a major culinary component for Feast Cafe Bistro chef and owner Christa Bruneau-Guenther. Before the colonial introduction of white sugar and flour, her ancestors used cattail or wild rice flour, sweetening it with berries or maple syrup and frying in animal fats, but these days, she chooses the easier more modern methodology and views bannock as a sign of resilience, survival and creativity. Like Mexican tacos, the toppings are up to you, but Bruneau-Guenther suggests shredded lettuce, dice red onion, shredded cheese, salsa and sour cream.

1. Heat the oil in a frying pan over medium heat. Add the onions and sauté for 3 minutes, until softened.

2. Add the bison and cook, breaking up the meat using a wooden spoon, for 2 minutes or until browned. Add the garlic and cook for another 1 minute.

3. Add the salt, chili powder, paprika, cumin and pepper, stirring to mix well.

4. Stir in the tomato sauce and maple syrup. Add the corn and beans. Simmer with the lid on to prevent splattering. Stir every few minutes until the mixture is well combined and heated through.

5. Spoon the mixture onto the warm fry bread tacos and garnish with your choice of toppings.

SERVES 4

1 to 2 Tbsp (15 to 30 ml) olive, vegetable or canola oil

1 onion, diced

1 pound (450 g) ground bison or beef

3 cloves garlic, minced

1 tsp (5 ml) kosher salt

1 tsp (5 ml) chili powder

1 tsp (5 ml) smoked paprika

½ tsp (2 ml) cumin powder

¼ tsp (1 ml) ground black pepper

1 (14 ounce/398 ml) can tomato sauce

2 Tbsp (30 ml) maple syrup, honey or brown sugar

½ cup (125 ml) frozen corn kernels

½ cup (125 ml) turtle beans (black beans) or any bean you like

Fry bread tacos (see page 285)

FRY BREAD TACOS

1. In large bowl or on clean work surface, combine the flour, baking powder and salt. Make a well in the middle of the dry ingredients and pour in the warm water and 2 Tbsp (30 ml) of the oil. Using a fork, spoon or your clean hands, work the dry ingredients into the liquid. Gently knead the dough into a ball, being careful to not over-knead.

2. Divide the dough into five or six evenly sized pieces. Cover with a clean kitchen towel.

3. Flatten the dough pieces on a floured work surface to ½ inch (1.2 cm) thick.

4. Pour the remaining 1 Tbsp (15 ml) of the oil into a deep frying pan and heat to about 350°F (175°C) (it will start shimmering). Add the dough pieces (you may need to work in batches). Fry for 3 to 4 minutes on each side, until crispy and browned. Transfer fry bread to plate lined with paper towel. Make sure to let the oil come back up to temperature in between batches.

MAKES 5 TO 6 FRY BREAD TACOS

3 cups (750 ml) unbleached all-purpose flour, plus extra for dusting

1 Tbsp (15 ml) baking powder

1 tsp (5 ml) kosher salt

1¼ cups (310 ml) warm water

3 Tbsp (45 ml) vegetable, canola or grapeseed oil, divided

Optional Toppings

Shredded lettuce

Diced red onions

Shredded cheddar cheese

Salsa

Sour cream

Chopped cilantro

Primal

SASKATOON, SASKATCHEWAN (2015–Present)

When Christie Peters and Kyle Michael opened Primal in 2015, they were toying with the idea of naming it Elevator, and while its current name suits the pared-down culinary mastery, the former would have been telling of the focus on grain at this restaurant. The cuisine is Italian, and

Beef Heart Bolognese, Primal

all the pasta is created with locally ground flour made with heritage grains grown in Saskatchewan, which Peters and Michael thought was the perfect way to showcase the bounty of the province's reputation as "breadbasket of the world." Whole-animal butchery is of equal importance here, as is locality and sustainability—all the kitchen scraps go into the compost for the gardens, which are overseen by the on-staff horticulturist who grows the restaurant's produce in the basement and in garden plots around the city.

Sitting at the long wooden communal table at the centre of the restaurant or cozied up on the wall banquettes, diners slurp up Red Fife spaghetti done aglio e olio–style, devour bison carpaccio or tagliatelle Bolognese made with locally pastured pork and beef heart, and swoon over risotto, the wild mushrooms bringing the umami.

Beef Heart Bolognese

Recipe from Primal

Chef Christie Peters is used to serving big numbers at her bustling Primal, and this is a recipe for a crowd. You'll need a meat grinder for it, but it's well worth the effort. Made with pork scrap and beef heart, this bolognese is right on brand with her advocacy of whole-animal butchery. After simmering this fragrant sauce on the stove, toss your favourite pasta into the pot and you've got a party.

1. Grind the beef and pork together in a meat grinder, then set aside. Grind the carrots, garlic and fennel together; set aside separately from the meat.

2. In a large braiser set over medium-high heat, sear the meat in small batches until caramelized. Strain the meat after each batch, reserving the fat that drains off.

3. When all the meat has been seared, add the fat back into the pan, along with the onions, carrots, garlic, and fennel, and cook over medium heat for about 5 minutes or until golden brown.

4. Once the vegetables have cooked down, stir in the tomato paste and cook for 5 minutes. Deglaze the pan with the wine, let cook for 1 to 2 minutes to cook off the alcohol, then return the meat to the pan.

5. Hand crush the tomatoes and add to the pan. Reduce the heat to low and cook for 1 hour. Season to taste with salt.

6. To serve, stir in the milk and butter, then add the Parmigiano-Reggiano to taste. Bring the mixture to a simmer before adding cooked pasta of your choice.

SERVES 8 TO 10

5 pounds (2.5 kg) beef heart or other cuts of beef

2 pounds (900 g) pork scrap, prosciutto or bacon

1 large carrot

¾ cup (180 ml) whole garlic cloves

8 ounces (250 g) frozen fennel tops or bulbs

2 onions, finely chopped

8 ounces (250 g) tomato paste

1 cup (250 ml) red wine

Two (3 L) cans whole tomatoes, hand crushed

Kosher salt

1 cup (250 ml) milk

2 Tbsp (30 ml) butter

Parmigiano-Reggiano, finely grated (almost powder-like), to taste

Cooked pasta of your choice, for serving

Semsem

OTTAWA, ONTARIO (2016–Present)

Fast-casual in its most accepted terms is ubiquitous in Canada, but on-demand baked goods? Not so much. At Semsem, the Levantine breads are made only once they're ordered. When Mayassaa Chaltaf and her brother-in-law, Mohamed Al-Abed, arrived in Canada in 2016, they opened a Palestinian breakfast and lunch spot called Semsem (Arabic for sesame) in a South Keys strip mall. They decided to showcase all of the Levantine breads, and I mean all of them. Man'ouche with za'atar comes out of the oven and to the table six at a time; loaves shaped into wreaths and stuffed with halloumi and dotted with sesame seeds arrive steaming, followed by fatteh, falafel and shakshouke, baked in the oven upon ordering.

Kuugaq Cafe

CAMBRIDGE BAY, NUNAVUT (2017–Present)

There are fewer than five restaurants (and no cafe or public space to hang out in) in Cambridge Bay, Canada's most northern community. It wasn't until the Canadian High Arctic Research Station opened in 2017 and brought an influx of visiting scientists and new residents that the opening of the Kuugaq Cafe was spurred along. Five shareholders opened the restaurant that very same year: Amanda Doiron-Rostant, Stuart Rostant, Mason Greenley, Ovi Evans, and Joel Evans, but it was Doiron-Rostant and Rostant who ran the show. The couple also owned the building, which houses their Ublu Inn and commercial office space.

Inside the cafe, exposed beams, local art hung on the walls, and a peaked ceiling with black vents give the place an urban feel like cafes in the south do. The menu is also decidedly urban, with coffees and baked goods and an ever-changing lunch offering, along with quinoa salads, poutines and burgers. Rostant is from Trinidad and hired his sister Helen as the cook, so there's an infusion of Caribbean too: think muskox pizza, and chicken swapped out for caribou in the Trinidadian stew.

The cafe closed during the first wave of COVID closures, but Marielle and Adrian Nocon (who both immigrated from the Philippines via a stint in Nova Scotia where they met) have since taken over, continuing to serve plates of pasta, burgers and arctic char chowder.

That's a Wrap

As the COVID-19 pandemic hit in early 2020 and shut down pretty much everything across the country, swinging a hard right hook to the restaurant industry, the contactless fast-casual Box'd chain opened in Toronto. A nouveau version of the automat with digitized cubby holes created by those behind Paramount Fine Foods, Box'd brought Middle Eastern dishes into a new contactless age. The automat was never as popular a trend in Canada as it was in the eastern United States in the first half of the 20th century, but it still evokes a confusing sense of nostalgia and the futuristic unknown in the restaurant industry. Which, even after more than two years of wave upon wave of epidemical upsurges, is still pretty darn uncertain.

I started writing *Where We Ate* when I was locked down in my house with my husband because of the global pandemic. As I sanitized my groceries and watched daily news reports, I realized the book would have to have a new chapter, and new perspective. I had grand visions of travelling the country, eating my way across the vast spaces. Instead, I spent hundreds

of hours on Zoom, chatting with restaurant owners, chefs and food writers about one of the things I love most: restaurants. And, boy, did the 2020s have a rocky start when it came to restaurants. At least 13 of those featured in this book closed due to COVID cruelties, and by the time the book is published, I am certain there will be more.

No one has a fortune cookie big enough to predict how the global pandemic has shifted Canada's restaurant industry, but one thing is for certain: restaurants aren't going anywhere. Patrons ordered takeout from their favourite restaurants weekly and bought gift cards to use in the future, and governments offered help keeping our favourite restaurants open during the darkest days of COVID-19.

On the Prairies, beloved fall suppers that usually take place in community halls, with diners eating together shoulder to shoulder at long tables while balanced on folding chairs, shifted to a drive-thru model to keep a hundred-year-old tradition and fundraiser alive. In Pansy Hall, Manitoba, the 2020 annual fall supper, usually a Ukrainian smorgasbord of fried chicken, cheddar and potato perogies, cabbage rolls and vegetables, was offered via takeout only. In Toronto, Allison Gibson turned her restaurant Paintbox Bistro into a grocery store to save employees' jobs and keep the lights on. Quebec City's Buffet Royal saw the resurgence of an old tradition: the drive-in, with eat-in-your-car curbside service. Owner Éric Sanfaçon saw a huge uptick in business as people relived the nostalgic 1950s—that bygone era in which the restaurant had opened—all the while supporting their favourite local restaurant.

Restaurants have taken hit after hit, forever adapting to the "new normal" with shifting regulations on masking, capacity and vaccination passports, and we lost some favourites across the country. But some brave entrepreneurs still opened in the middle of a global disaster. Just like during the Great Depression and both World Wars, people still dined out and still opened restaurants. Our love for communal eating eclipses whatever is going on in the world the minute we break bread, even if it's just for a few bites. In Cape Breton, the small town of Sydney River welcomed a new dim sum restaurant called Super Bun in 2021. Co-owner Dean Liu and his family moved from Hong Kong to Cape Breton and are now serving buns, dumplings and egg-custard tarts.

And one of the first things most people did as restrictions loosened up? They ate at their favourite restaurant. It felt good to dine out again. A quick weeknight meal at the local brasserie with your spouse, a formal dinner with your girlfriends to celebrate an engagement, or takeout sushi in the park with your dog—these experiences aren't going anywhere.

What we eat will certainly change, with the rise of plant-based cuisine and the impact of meat consumption on climate change, but where we eat more than likely will not. When it comes down to it, Canadian cuisine is a delicious mix of global influence and local ingredients, and what makes it the most special is that it's enjoyed by everyone. We will continue to try new restaurants, take photos of our food and remember where we ate.

Acknowledgements

When I first saw the designed pages for *Where We Ate*, I welled up. My husband, Adam, so poignantly (and hilariously) said: "It's like the ultrasound for your book!" and he was so right. Writing this book was a labour of love, and of drudgery, but as I talked about in my introduction, this was a true passion project for me. A love letter to all those times I have spent in restaurants with the people I love—my happiest memories with my parents, with my coworkers, and with my best friends took place in a restaurant. And I'm so thankful to all the chefs, restaurant owners, and restaurant lovers who helped me put *Where We Ate* out into the world.

I mostly have Adam to thank for pretty much everything in my life, but in particular, for your patience, guidance, and constant hunger while writing this book. Thank you for being my editor, my roommate, my travel buddy, my forever partner in dine. I knew we were meant to be when our banter (and wine consumption) closed out a restaurant when we were first dating.

Family and friends have always been first in my life, and I want to thank all of you who didn't mind so much when *Where We Ate* took centre stage for the better part of two years. My parents, Cathy and Dan, who are my ceaseless cheerleaders and my dear sissy Maggie who birthed my beautiful niece Sloane while I was birthing this book.

My dear friends—the Clam Rims, the Jade Rollers, and the Girlies—you know who you are. Thank you for always supporting my rollercoaster of a life and making me feel loved.

Where We Ate would be nowhere at all without the whole team at Appetite by Random House! My eternal gratitude to my editor, Zoe, for the pep talks and for making me feel like a legit author. To Robert, the publisher who took an offhand idea and helped make this book a reality by hounding me for years until I was able to defeat my imposter syndrome and send him a book proposal—you saw what my writing could be. To Colin, for his constant appreciation of restaurant criticism and for spearheading the Literary Annoyers Club, tracking down imagery for the book. And to Emma—I've already talked about your design making me cry. Thank you for your hard work to make this book so beautiful.

I so appreciated chatting with all the food writers, bloggers, and fellow critics across the country who offered insight into the dining scene in their neck of the woods: Lindsay Anderson, Julian Armstrong, John Atkin, Jennifer Bain, Alex Bialek, Melissa Buote, Twyla Campbell, Lesley Chesterman, Elizabeth Chorney-Booth, Dan Clapson, Nathalie Cooke, Ilona Daniels, Helen Earley, Heidi Fink, Diane Galambos, Alexandra Gill, Michele Genest, Mike Green, Naomi Hansen, Renée Kohlman, Tiffany Mayer, Corey Mintz, Chris Nuttall-Smith, Amy Pataki, Karen Pinchin, Katherine Romanow, Allison Saunders, Jenn Sharp, Jay Smith, Mia Stainsby, Simon Thibault, Dana Van-Veller, Jan Wong, and Shel Zolkewich.

I want to say a special thank you to all the archivists across this country, especially those who keep the museums, university collections, and archives of small towns running—you keep the history and memory of Canada's restaurants alive. I chatted with so many of you across the country who helped me so enthusiastically. I can never repay you.

A special note to my father-in-law who passed away before this book went to press. He so wanted to see my name in bookstores, and though he forever claimed he wasn't a picky eater—he really was. My greatest regret is not connecting the dots between "that Afghan restaurant Andy (my brother-in-law) took us to in Vancouver," where he so bravely tried new dishes and the fact that it was, indeed, the Afghan Horsemen which is featured in this book, where the Ronan family toasted him last May. Cheers, Gerry.

Photo Credits

FRONTMATTER

Title page: "Dining at Banff Springs Hotel, Banff, Alberta.", [ca. 1924], (CU1123987) by Brigden's Studios. Courtesy of Libraries and Cultural Resources Digital Collections, University of Calgary.
Dedication page: Courtesy of Au Pied de Cochon
Have a seat: Taiwan Restaurant; Gabby Peyton, Headshot; Alex Stead

CHAPTER 1: BEFORE CONFEDERATION

Chapter opener: William Coopers Coffee House; Library and Archives Canada, accession 1970-188-2092 W.H. Coverdale Collection of Canadiana
Auberge Saint Gabriel; Auberge Saint Gabriel; Recipe Image: Auberge Saint Gabriel
King's Head Inn; Artist Owen Staples, courtesy of Toronto Public Library JRR 3278/PICTURES-R-125
Restaurant Compain; McCord Museum M984.203.5
The Windsor House Hotel; City of Ottawa Archives MG393-NP-49569-001 CA044241
Six Mile Pub; Six Mile Pub
Stewart's Dining Room & Oyster Saloon; Recipe Image: Gabby Peyton
The Pioneer Hotel; University of British Columbia Library Rare Books and Special Collections BC-403

CHAPTER 2: CONFEDERATION TO 1910

Chapter opener: "Banff Springs Hotel, Banff, Alberta.", [ca. 1910], (CU1172158) by Unknown. Courtesy of Libraries and Cultural Resources Digital Collections, University of Calgary.
Washington's Restaurant; Provincial Archives of New Brunswick, P210-2732
Joe's Juneau; Dawson City Museum, Front Street Dawson, July 1899, 2011.14.24

Glacier House; Glenbow Archives NA-1608-5
Banff Springs Hotel; Banff Springs Hotel
Chateau Frontenac; Courtesy of Fairmont Chateau Frontenac
McAdam Railway Station; Jason Bennett
Royal Alexandra Hotel; The Canadian Railroad Historical Association/Exporail, Canadian Pacific Railway Company Fonds P170-A-9834-300PPP
The Empress Hotel, Afternoon Tea outside the Empress; Fairmont Empress Hotel; Recipe image: Gabby Peyton
Cafe Aagaard; Lawrence Stuckey fonds (1-2002.3.1E9), SJ McKee Archives, Brandon University
Wood's Candy and Fruit Store and Restaurant; Photo #01-23-007: City of St. John's Archives

CHAPTER 3: THE 1910s

Chapter opener: Courtesy of Port Dover Harbour Museum 2019.25.8 Arbor Exterior
Club Cafe; Glenbow Archives NA-2768-5
Montreal Pool Room; Melissa Hartfiel
United Bakers Dairy; United Bakers Dairy
The Rex Hotel; The Rex Hotel
Green Lantern; E.A. Bollinger Nova Scotia Archives 1975-305 1941 no. 234a
Union Cafe; Glenbow Archives PA-3685-26
Hoito; Archives & Digital Collections at Lakehead University Library scan #270219-002; MG3, Box 1, File 13, Item 14 scan #101007-001
Mel's Tea Room; Mount Allison University Archives—8001/198; Mount Allison University Archives—2007.11
The Arbor; Courtesy of Port Dover Harbour Museum 2019.25.4 Arbor Staff Exterior

CHAPTER 4: THE 1920s

Chapter opener: Kate Aitken with unnamed students. Exhibition Place Records & Archives

Johnson's Cafe; City of Edmonton Archives EA-10-100

Sid Beech's Tamale Parlor; Museum of Vancouver Collection H2006.55.32

Georgian Room, Eaton's; Ontario Archives T. Eaton Fonds F 229-308-0-2308-1

Schwartz's; Guilhem Vellut

White Spot; White Spot

The Senator; The Senator

Sooke Harbour House; Sooke Region Museum and Visitor Centre SRHS#1609

CHAPTER 5: THE 1930s

Chapter opener: Salisbury House

Gem Cafe; A-1855 courtesy of Saskatoon Public Library

Salisbury House; Salisbury House

Old Spain; PEI Museums Postcard Collection, a cooperative project of the PEI Museum and Heritage Foundation and the UPEI Robertson Library

Green Door; Al Harvey; City of Vancouver Archives, CVA 260-1545, photographer James Crookall

Java Shop; Courtesy of The Culinary Institute of America Menu Collection, Conrad N. Hilton Library, Hyde Park, N.Y.

Wildcat Cafe; Glenbow Archives NA-3873-8

Moishes; Moishes

CHAPTER 6: THE 1940s

Chapter opener: Norman's Restaurant menu, 19 October 1943, H.B. Jefferson Nova Scotia Archives

The Chickenburger; The Chickenburger

Chan's Restaurant of Distinction; PEI Museums Postcard Collection, a cooperative project of the PEI Museum and Heritage Foundation and the UPEI Robertson Library

Toad River Lodge; Toad River Lodge

Pizzeria Napoletana; Pizzeria Napoletana

Round Up Cafe; City of Surrey Archives, F83-0-0-0-0-0-0-37

CHAPTER 7: THE 1950s

Chapter opener: Chi Gardens Menu, 1950s. University of Toronto Scarborough Library, Archives & Special Collections, Harley J. Spiller Collection, Menus from Canada—Saskatchewan.

Joe's Lunch; LH-8706 courtesy of Saskatoon Public Library

Ches's Famous Fish and Chips; Ches's Famous Fish and Chips

Roma Bakery & Deli; Roma Bakery & Deli

The Paddlewheel; Hudson's Bay Company Archives, Archives of Manitoba HBCA 1987/363-W-325/27

Foo's Ho Ho; Gunter Marx/Alamy Stock Photo; City of Vancouver Archives, CVA 70-68, photographer Art Grice

Junior's; Junior's

Marie Antoinette Restaurant & Tahiti Bar; Recipe Image: Gabby Peyton; styling by Kris Smith

New Glasgow Lobster Suppers; New Glasgow Lobster Suppers

CHAPTER 8: THE 1960s

Chapter opener: Courtesy of Walter Craft Caesar

Satellite Restaurant; Chatham-Kent Museum 1985.27.6.63; North side of King Street between Fourth St. and Fifth St., Chatham, Ontario; shows Satellite Restaurant, Boyes & Herd, Corner Furniture, Lambton Trust and Loan. Book 6, No. 63, Frank H. Brown Collection.

Bill Wong's; Courtesy of Jan and Julie Wong

The Coffee Mill; Bob Olsen/Toronto Star via Getty Images Image #:528456644

Le Roy Jucep; Gabby Peyton

Tim Hortons; Tim Hortons

Moskva at Expo 67; Library and Archives Canada 4943977

The Naam; City of Vancouver Archives,
CVA 780-193
Mary Brown's; Mary Brown's

CHAPTER 9: THE 1970s
Chapter opener: Buffet, CP-9000-5 courtesy
of Saskatoon Public Library
Houston Pizza; Nicole Harling
Gourmet Fare at Sherway Gardens; Copyright
© 1979-2021 Robert Lansdale Photography
and Robert C. Lansdale. All Rights Reserved.
Fat Frank's; Doug Griffin / Toronto Star via
Getty Images Image #502324693
Afghan Horsemen; Gabby Peyton
The Silver Inn Restaurant; Elyse Bouvier
Richard's Fresh Seafood; Richard's Fresh Seafood
King of Donair; King of Donair
Le Saint-Amour; Kamarad
Korean Village Restaurant; Korean Village
Restaurant

CHAPTER 10: THE 1980s
Chapter opener: BeaverTails
BeaverTails; Duo-Tang Studio
Lotus; Kid Lee
Tojo's; Tojo's; Recipe Image: Tojo's

CHAPTER 11: THE 1990s
Chapter opener: courtesy of Toqué!
North 44; The McEwan Group
River Café; Pauline Yu Photography;
Recipe Image: Pauline Yu Photography
Thi Thi Vietnamese Submarine; Ken Lee
Toqué!; Hans Laurendeau and Shoot Studio
Vij's; Jeremy Koreski
Max & Moritz Spicy Island Food House;
Max & Moritz Spicy Island Food House
Liliget Feast House; Liliget Feast House
The Pointe Restaurant at Wickaninnish Inn;
Jeremy Koreski

Chez Christophe; Steve Bly/Alamy Stock Photo
Image ID: BH6M4J
Kintaro Ramen; Gabby Peyton

CHAPTER 12: THE 2000s
Chapter opener: Japadog
Au Pied Du Cochon; André-Olivier Lyra
Grassmere Family Restaurant; Grassmere Family
Restaurant
D Hot Shoppe; D Hot Shoppe
Japadog; Japadog
The Star Cafe; The Star Cafe
Black Hoof; Daniel Neuhaus
Tacofino; Melissa Hartfiel (truck) and
Gabby Peyton (tacos)

CHAPTER 13: THE 2010s
Chapter opener: Courtesy of Sweet Jesus, Toronto
Grumman 78; Mickaël A. Bandassak
Harvest Eatery; Chris Attrell
Mallard Cottage; Anja Sajovic Photography
Bite House; Bite House; Recipe Image: Bite House
Les Brumes du Coude; Les Brumes du Coude
Wayfarer Oyster House; Maude Chauvin
Primal; Primal; Recipe image: Primal
Fireworks Feast, Inn at Bay Fortune; Fireworks
Feast, Inn at Bay Fortune
Feast Cafe Bistro; Feast Cafe Bistro
Semsem; Semsem

Index